T0354635

Consider the Raven

Meditations Beside a Vernal Pool

VIRGINIA REYNOLDS WILLIAMS

WESTBOW
PRESS®
A DIVISION OF THOMAS NELSON
& ZONDERVAN

WestBow Press books may be ordered through booksellers or by contacting:

WestBow Press
A Division of Thomas Nelson & Zondervan
1663 Liberty Drive
Bloomington, IN 47403
www.westbowpress.com
1 (866) 928-1240

Because of the dynamic nature of the Internet, any web addresses or
links contained in this book may have changed since publication and
may no longer be valid. The views expressed in this work are solely those
of the author and do not necessarily reflect the views of the publisher,
and the publisher hereby disclaims any responsibility for them.

Any people depicted in stock imagery provided by Getty Images are
models, and such images are being used for illustrative purposes only.
Certain stock imagery © Getty Images.

Scripture taken from the King James Version of the Bible.

ISBN: 978-1-9736-5490-2 (sc)
ISBN: 978-1-9736-5492-6 (hc)
ISBN: 978-1-9736-5491-9 (e)

Library of Congress Control Number: 2019902208

Print information available on the last page.

WestBow Press rev. date: 2/25/2019

To Tony, whose words "Where did you get your love for God and your love for birds?" kept me going when I would have given up.

CONTENTS

Dry Season

L ove of nature, love of the Word of God, and the relevance of both in our daily lives are what these meditations seek to demonstrate. Birdlife and drama are reflected on as the seasons change around the vernal pool: from a lake teeming with flocks of birds in winter to a dry field of grass in summer where birds stay hidden. Is the California drought playing a role here? Maybe that's why there are more predators (hawks and ravens) this year. The threatening wildfires serve as reminders of the fragility of life and suggest end-time warnings.

Some small finches just banded with a mockingbird to chase a hawk away. The Bible warns of "false prophets" and that they are "among us," not in the enemy camp. There is no blinking red light to tell us who they are. We have to be alert, as the birds, for when we think it's safe and quiet, the threat descends like a hawk.

These thoughts seek to elevate the work of the Creator and the message He gives through creation, along with His written Word. Keeping always in mind: "The fashion of this world passeth away" (1 Corinthians 7:31) and "The grass withereth, the flower fadeth, but the Word of our God shall stand forever" (Isaiah 40:8). His Word is eternal, though even "the heavens shall pass away" (2 Peter 3:10). We need to give urgent heed to this Word that is eternal (Hebrews 2:1) as we observe His temporal handwork.

He did tell us to "consider the ravens" (Luke 12:24), and throughout scripture are mentioned object lessons in nature of deeper truths contained in His written Word.

Among things considered here are issues in our world and culture today, intertwining bird observations and scripture to help give an insightful perspective on an issue that only may *seem* new because it's being experienced by someone for the first time. The issue itself may be as old as the Garden of Eden.

Looking at the beauty, harmony, and order of creation—even in a polluted, decaying world—helps the observer sort thoughts and get a better perspective on issues we face in our troubled, darkening world.

WET SEASON

Bird-Watching with God

Bird-watching is something I do with God. Though I do it more often and more knowledgeably than some people, what I see does not compare to what the ornithologist, the specialized photographer, or even the dedicated bird-watcher sees. And none do it as well as God, who does not forget a single sparrow (Luke 12:6). I watch two house sparrows zig and zag in flight together and wonder what they are doing. Playing? Fighting? Mating? Then they are out of sight, and I have no more knowledge of their tussle. But not God. He still watches them and will see the outcome of this little soap opera.

But I got to see part of it! More than those hurrying to class, back to their apartments, or off to work, I was the one who got my spirits lifted from the problems of this earth for a few moments, to consider the awesomeness of life around me that goes on beautifully whether I notice it or not. Then the birds were gone, reminding me that I have other problems to turn my mind to. God will take care of the birds, and He will take care of me and my problems too.

CHAPTER 2

My New Binocs!

My new binoculars are marvelous! Before, I could only tell by their quick, loopy flight patterns that these birds were swallows. But now, I can occasionally see colors and markings. They are still pretty quick, but I can tell a Tree Swallow from a Violet-green Swallow. Sometimes. But I can't quite tell the juvenile Tree Swallow from a Bank Swallow. Before these binocs, I couldn't see any of the defining details at any time. Now, I see more—and I know what to look for.

In addition to details of individual birds, I can see details on the far shore of the vernal pool that I couldn't see before. One day in the rain, I saw a little troop of Tree Swallows lined up on the wire of the fence like soldiers. Pointing this out to someone beside me, he just gave me a blank stare and a polite nod. Of course! He didn't have my binoculars. That was why he couldn't see what was so clear to me. Not long ago, I couldn't have seen it either.

The Bible is like binoculars for life. Knowing it enables us to see details and make sense of the blurry whir of life around us. What is sometimes obvious to one who reads his or her Bible is a mystery to one who does not. Therefore, we who read must be patient as we share with others the joys, insights, and warnings God has given. They may not have the binoculars we have or not yet be as skilled at focusing, finding, and moving with fluid motion with the Word.

Of course, there are some problems with these new binoculars. Actually, not with the binoculars but with the one using them.

Sometimes I get tunnel vision as I focus on one bird, trying to identify it, and I don't see the Bald Eagle circling and swooping down to snatch the little Bufflehead. Missing part of the big picture is not the fault of the binoculars. I've got to remember to keep checking the big picture even while I focus on a detail.

God's Word can be misread, misinterpreted, and misapplied by humans using it to back up some view they want to expound. The Word is still God's and true—even if humans misuse and misunderstand it.

CHAPTER 3

Going by the Book

There's nothing like using the senses God gave you to tell you what you are seeing. However, sometimes these senses and the database they are connected to (your own brain) just aren't enough. We underestimate and overestimate this brain all the time and will never fully appreciate it until we've lost it. We do need other sources of information to help us figure out life.

Did I just see a female Bullock's Oriole—or did a Western Tanager flit by? This is when I need more than my brain and the memories stored there. I need my bird handbook or the bird app on my Android tablet. As I thumb through the pages of a book, I'm absorbing information—even if it's not what I'm seeking right now—that will help in future identifications. The bird app on my Android helps for quick spot IDs and confirmation of sightings, but it's not quite the solid foundation the handbook is. In fairness to the app, though, I must admit that I am a book-oriented person and biased to begin with.

The Bible is the handbook for life. We read parts that don't seem relevant to us at the moment; perhaps they are not the answer to a particular problem we are facing. But the information is planted in our brains, and it clicks together with meaning at a future significant time. How tedious is reading the law of the Old Testament. Then we read in the New Testament: "By the law is the knowledge of sin" (Romans 3:20). That's how we know we are sinners and need the grace of God.

Cathedrals of the Forest

How amiable are thy tabernacles
O LORD of hosts!
My soul longeth, yea fainteth for the courts of the LORD:
My heart and my flesh cry out for the living God.
Yea, the sparrow hath found an house,
And the swallow a nest for herself,
Where she may lay her young,
Even thine altars,
O LORD of hosts,
My King and my God.
—Psalm 84

The tabernacles of Psalm 84 are like the cathedrals of the forest: an audience always raising its arms to praise the LORD. Certainly the heart and the flesh long for this place of peace, in the awesome presence of the Designer. Here in the arms of the forest are found the altars: the young in the nests laid before the Lord of hosts.

The vernal pool has small groves of oak trees on two sides. Highways lock these in. As much as I would like to picture the quiet peace of a forest of evergreens, these scraggly oaks that lose their garments in fall will have to suffice. They do lift their arms, and though I haven't trekked through them looking for bird nests, it makes me think all the more that these nests are there, undisturbed by humans.

I did find the nest of a Lark Sparrow one day; its masklike face blinked at my binoculars from its grassy nest above me in an oak.

This was her altar to the LORD.

CHAPTER 5

To Kill a Mockingbird

Pulling into the college parking lot, I take note of the first birds I see. I groan as the familiar mockingbird begins his welcome repertoire. Yesterday, that bird did not shut up, and the title of *To Kill a Mockingbird* kept going through my head. I used to wonder why anyone would think of doing such a thing. I wonder no more.

As I make my way around the campus, getting the big picture of what birds might be here today, that mockingbird doesn't stop annoying me. Certainly he is not the same one I had thought of as a friend who would land in the bush beside my car when I arrived and then hop from tree to tree until I sat down on my usual bench by the front door. Then, from the top of the oak in front of me, he would warble his repertoire to all who could hear. One sounded like a parrot: "Pretty bird. Pretty bird." Another sounded like a House Finch chattering. That's how I knew him: his repertoire.

After I went inside the building, I would see him again when I stepped outside the west door to pick up the newspaper. The repertoire would start again. One time, my husband picked me up from work, and my mockingbird was hopping around the trees in the parking lot, seemingly trying to follow the car as we left.

"He's in love with you," my husband said with a chuckle.

Since then, I've noticed other mockingbirds with different repertoires. One sounded like a car alarm going off.

I do a quick walk around the campus, confirming there are two separate flocks of Greater White-fronted Geese at different ends of the education building. I see one of the college boys chasing a pair of Canada Geese from the grass beside the parking lot back to the vernal pool. I'll have to speak to him.

CHAPTER 6

No Teacher Like Observation

There is no teacher like observation. But, sometimes, what you think you see is not what is really there. So you need the help of another's eyes. Does that person see it too? Then a third pair of eyes really confirms the issue. But what if all are deceived by what they collectively agree on? It happens in politics, science, and narratives of war (to name a few subjects).

It's certainly true in observations of birds, insects, and animals. Who would know the bird better: the one who memorized the description from a handbook or the one who watched it every day? But just watching it is not enough. The observer only sees the bird in that small range of his or her binoculars or eyes. The range that little bird can cover quickly, either vertically or horizontally (or both), is certainly faster and farther than the human eye can go, even with binoculars. The human observer, too, is limited, fastened to the ground by gravity. Sure, gravity affects the bird, but it doesn't limit him. Drones might be useful, but I don't think birds would like them. I'll have to look into that.

As it is, birds just remind us of our limitations, even our limited powers of observation. Even with binoculars, telescopes, and microscopes, we are limited. Every invention reveals more limitations we weren't aware of before.

CHAPTER 7

Don't Belittle Your Own Observation

If the text said, "Birds cannot fly," yet I saw a bird fly, would not my observation prove a better teacher than the text? At this point, I will seek a different text to instruct me, one that does not contradict my own observations.

But I want to understand things beyond what my own observations are limited to. At which point I have two choices: accept the observations of another or commence my own speculation. A combination of all the above is a good practice.

The observations of another fall into two categories: word of mouth or documented research.

Word of mouth. Do I trust the person who is telling me his observation of a bird? If he's someone who lives in the country or is a hunter, then I will accept his observations of birds of the wild, comparing my stories to his while learning a little more.

Can observation be faulty? If I never observed a bird flying higher than an oak tree, and thus concluded that no bird could fly that high, I'd be wrong. I'd have exalted the power of my observation too high. I need to compare my observations with others. We will pool our knowledge and see what conclusions we can draw. Or seek the observations of noted ornithologists who have written on the subject and know what even other authorities have to say. Of course, even a noted, educated authority can be wrong. The final judge is my own observation, so I must never dismiss it.

The heavens declare the glory of God ... day unto
day uttereth speech ... there is no language where
their voice is not heard. (Psalm 19:1--3)

God spoke through His creation to all men. Not just to
theologians, priests, and religious people, but to all: high and
mighty, low and helpless. Anyone who can look at and appreciate
nature has no excuse. He has heard the voice of God (Romans
1:19–20)

Observing nature causes us to question more and more things
we see in this world around us. Where is that bird going? Why is
its mouth open? How can birds tell each other apart when they
all look alike? On and on. Sometimes answers are found, but then
questions multiply faster than the answers coming in. It makes us
aware of the immeasurable immensity of the knowledge we do not
have and could not assimilate if we could begin to tap into it. Where
is this knowledge? No library is big enough to hold it all. Efficient
computers are being developed, but they can't hold the knowledge
that hasn't yet been discovered. What has been discovered is only
an infinitesimal speck in the immeasurable universe of what can
be and cannot be known.

Even in light of this, each human continues to see himself or
herself as the center of the universe, to believe that their views are
the right ones, and will not cede any ground to another without an
argument, if even then.

I began this meditation by exalting the powers of human
observation, questioning them, and then finally trying to silence
them.

But why would God give His Word or speak through the
heavens (Psalm 19) if He hadn't expected us to consider, question,
and meditate? So we do need our powers of observation, as limited
and prone to error as they are.

CHAPTER 8

Drama on the Vernal Pool

Those who only contemplate birds at feeders in the safety of their backyards do not see the whole drama and danger in the bird's life. The innocent little Bufflehead, like a child in a pool, paddling around with his partner, then taking a dive under the surface. He goes totally under, not like the Mallard who leaves his tail in the air to show when he is probing underwater. All you can see of the Bufflehead on the water are the rings where he went under. The Bald Eagle has been circling above. Suddenly he dives, snatches the Bufflehead's partner, and is gone. When Bufflehead surfaces, he paddles in circles for a while, wondering where his partner went.

Viewing this as a mother, I think, *What a sad end to a little duck's life—to simply be a meal for a greedy raptor.* But that's not a fair judgment. How do I know the duck cares how long his life is? He obviously enjoyed what life he had. Then, as a mother, I see my children out on the vernal pool of life, the easy objects of some evil predator of this world. Or worse yet, that they themselves might be that bully or predator.

The parent must pause and remember who is in control. The script of our children's lives is not written by us or even by them. As much as we want to guide and control, and they want to break away, it is still God who is in control. But that doesn't mean we shrug our shoulders and cast them to the wind.

Prayer is still our most powerful tool, and God does answer in His way in His time. So when we put our children in the hand of God, we remember: "It is a fearful thing to fall into the hands of the living God" (Hebrews 10:31).

CHAPTER 9

Letter to My Best Friend—or Betrayed

Note: another meditation neither about the vernal pool or birds—but thoughts I sorted out while beside the pool.

Through my long life, there have been many people who have fit the role of "best friend." The Lord brought our paths together, then parted them for one reason or another, and we both went on to seek other friends and be a friend somewhere else.

A friend is always there for unburdening woes and problems, or rejoicing in good times. Their view is valued as thoughts are bounced back and forth and opinions formed. We try to see ourselves through each other's eyes. Hopefully we got confirmation of what we wanted to see. If we don't get that confirmation, we figure out how to adjust.

It is important that this friend be honest and trustworthy. Someone only pretending to be a friend could do much harm.

So now, as I think on our friendship, my friend, I thank you for playing the role of God in my life for a short time. He used you to comfort, strengthen, and encourage me. Then, lest I depend on you too much, He allowed you to let me down, that I might learn to trust Him more.

That you let me down was not your fault. Though it hurt at the time, and I did bear a grudge that I had a hard time getting over, all is forgiven now in the light of that blessedness that only comes from growing in Christ as one difficult hurdle in life is finally passed.

Now other troubles wait, bigger than what has passed, and though I am stronger now than I was before, I know that only the Lord is the one to lean on.

Presumptive I have been to tell you that I forgive you for something you didn't even know you did! In the same token, I ask forgiveness for some way I may have wronged you and had no idea that I did. So, you may have already learned not to have too high an opinion of me. Hopefully, it hasn't turned you away from the church (that is happening much now days), but has caused you to look to the Lord and see Him in a new, fresh way, not stained by misconceptions, errors, or ignorance.

The old hymn "What a Friend We Have in Jesus" comes to mind. Human friends do let us down, even unintentionally. There is only that one Friend who is always there, whether in front of us to lead, beside us to encourage, or behind us to uphold or pick up. A fall is something you don't plan on or expect. It happens so quickly, and sometimes we knock others down when we fall. Injuries are caused that need attention and time to heal.

How wondrous to have that Friend who stands beside us through this recovery process. Why would anyone want to dare this rough road of life without Him?

CHAPTER 10
When to Speak

You can't say everything to everybody, but you must say something to somebody. But what to say and to whom? So, nothing is said to anyone.

Who needs to know something I can tell them and benefit from it? I must decide what I can say that is edifying and beneficial to someone else, then find a way to communicate it directly or indirectly. I don't need to worry if *everyone* needs to hear this. Just one.

Saying too much can be a great danger. Being bored, offended, or driven away are often the results of a rattling, unchecked, one-sided conversation in which one party wants to be understood but doesn't care if they understand the other.

God's purpose in His Holy Word was to say what was necessary. If all the details of every account had been written out, even the world itself could not contain the books that should be written. God wants us to get the basics.

This is the example I seek to follow as I write, fighting the urge to say everything I can and only say what is urgent, necessary, and edifying.

When I want life to be a quiet retreat to my library cave (where I am in control and everything is where it should be), suddenly it can turn into a carnival. Unexpected people make unexpected demands, assuming it is my job to serve them whenever they want me whatever their need. I accept that and move forward, reminding myself that I am not in control, but I know Who is.

The Tower of Babel is what I kept thinking of: how the language was confounded and the people couldn't understand each other. Here in America, people speak the same language and don't understand each other. The gaps relate to technology, generations, and countless culture gaps beyond male and female and everything in between and all around.

But probably the main reason people don't understand each other is they just don't listen to each other. This is a two-way street. Not just saying, "You must listen to me," but "I listen to you too."

CHAPTER II

Can We Overcome When Overwhelmed?

Sometimes people and life can be overwhelming. Scrolling through Facebook, you see face after face of all kinds of people, all ages, many nationalities representing countless causes, purposes, contemporary issues, and historical ones. This should get anyone out of "the-world-revolves-around-me" rut.

This multitude of people we are just skimming the surface of is itself but a grain of sand on a vast shore, each grain of which is different and unique. There are no two who look exactly alike or think exactly alike.

It reminds me again of how limited we humans are. One person cannot as efficiently handle life alone as one who has a partner to help. God divided the race into male and female, and through history, the two have divided their responsibilities according to each's strengths and weaknesses, thus accomplishing more together than either could alone (supposedly). But a mate isn't quite enough, so we're given kids to educate us (though we think we're educating them). Sometimes we learn; sometimes we don't. We think we are training these children, but they teach us unknowingly far more than we teach them. We learn things about ourselves as we watch them, we get a better perspective on relations with other people if our minds are open enough, and we're not spending so much time yelling we cannot hear. Then comes the time when the kids break away and go on their own life journeys with the limited tools we have equipped them with. They will need other tools, which they'll pick up along the way. Some of the tools that we gave them, which we thought were so essential, they'll have tossed aside as useless. Time will tell what was essential.

Now, back to each of us alone. Our journey isn't over yet. We've got a goal in mind, but will we be able to reach it? Many of the companions we chose to travel with have gone on other trails, though in the same direction, like the different routes of wagon trains going west across North America. Sometimes we cross paths again (like at a difficult mountain pass), compare notes and experiences, and give advice to each other. For some, we just want to put on a show, brag of our exploits, see our successes, and pretend there were no failures.

Failures are so painful. We pretend they don't happen to us. Ignore them. Focus our eyes on loftier things, as if the victory of the Seattle Seahawks could somehow be ours. That composition of Handel's, which we know so much about, becomes our accomplishment because we understand it better than anyone else we know. When our children accomplish something, we revel in it as if it were our own achievement. But when they fail, that, too, is our failure.

What are we to do? How can we handle failure? Many simply ignore it, and it stays like an ugly blot on their lives. That doesn't make it go away.

Alcoholics Anonymous has a principle of recognizing weakness so that it does not become a perpetual blot on life. As one "addict" quoted to me, "Recognizing we're powerless, that we have no control over the outcome no matter how hard we try, is step one."

That is the first step toward overcoming.

CHAPTER 12

Threatening Storm

Thoughts have been blowing through my mind like the storm clouds now blowing over the vernal pool, the oaks around it, and the distant mountains. It could almost put me to sleep, but the fluttering twigs of the old weeping willow seem to call to me: "Rise! Rise! There is work to do before the storm hits!"

Will the storm hit with fury, or will the winds die down, the clouds evaporate, and a sunny pleasant day invite us to play? Why work?

A threatening storm does remind us that time and life are short. If my own life doesn't end today, someone else's will, and I don't know if I might be their last contact with truth. My mother in a nursing home led her roommate to the Lord one evening. The next morning, that roommate was dead. Mom was thankful she hadn't put off sharing the gospel, and I'm sure that roommate was also.

CHAPTER 13

Knowing Nature, Knowing God

Is there a deeper truth that marriage and family are the object lessons of? Is it not the picture of a relationship and intimacy with God?

In a marriage, you get no more than you give. Those who neglect and abuse this relationship will get nothing from it. The same occurs in a relationship with God: "Ye shall seek me and find me when ye shall search for me with all your heart" (Jeremiah 29:13).

This is beyond just love. God gives His love, and there is nothing we can do to earn it. But there is a deeper relationship Paul spoke of: "That I may know Him, and the power of His resurrection, and the fellowship of His sufferings" (Philippians 3:10).

Some would equate an intimacy with nature as an intimacy with God. The heavens do "declare the glory of God and the firmament showeth His handiwork," but they are not God. That being said, they are His declaration, and knowing someone's works is a way to know them. Someone who despises what another person says cannot get to know them. Someone who loves nature but has no time for God's written Word cannot know Him as the one who loves His Word can know Him.

"Heaven and earth shall pass away, but my words shall not pass away" (Luke 21:33). From a human perspective, what could be more permanent than the stars of the heavens or the earth we stand on? Yet these shall pass away, we are told. What is eternal is this Book that has been outlawed, banned, burned, thrown away, and ignored by most of Earth's population.

These eternal words are what I want to share with any who will hear.

CHAPTER 14

Don't Be a Sitting Duck

What are the secrets to fighting an unseen enemy? Is it even possible? He has the first advantage, for he has you targeted, especially if you deny he exists, or refuse to acknowledge him; he calls the shots.

One trick of the enemy is disguise. Soldiers aren't alarmed when someone in their own uniform approaches. Satan is transformed as an angel of light (2 Corinthians 11:14). Satan? If you believe, like some, that Satan is just a thing made up by Christians, then you've already given him the upper hand in the offensive.

The term *sitting duck* certainly has a meaning for me now that it didn't before. As I pulled into the parking lot beside the vernal pool, a huge Bald Eagle was rising, descending, and swooping around, then descending again on a little flock of helpless ducks. He snatched the female Bufflehead, and after his attack, he went to the oaks on the far side of the pool with his prey. Not even a single Mallard was still in the pool. They had deserted their little friends. One lone male Bufflehead paddled around. The geese haven't been there for several days. Even the local starlings, pigeons, and Western Bluebirds are not in sight. Or the mockingbird and his noisy cousins, the Scrub Jays.

Probably not attractive to the eagle are those small birds, like sparrows, finches, and swallows that are quicker than the eagle and sometimes band together to chase him out of their territory.

Being small, they probably don't offer much of a meal, so the eagle won't bother.

But those clumsy ducks are stuck on the water like a target. Though they can fly, they do seem more awkward and clumsy than even the larger geese, who are slow and graceful and fly in unity in large numbers. But that's just my conclusions, which could be wrong. Ducks may not be the most helpless bird, it just seems that way. Where else would the expression "sitting duck" come from if there weren't sitting ducks?

Satan is being transformed as an angel of light, and so are his ministers (2 Corinthians 11:14). Ministers? So, there's more than just one evil force. How many are there? How much of a threat are they? Here is that unseen enemy in disguise. How on earth do we fight it?

"We wrestle not against flesh and blood, but against principalities, powers, the rulers of the darkness of this world, against spiritual wickedness in high places" (Ephesians 6:12). That sounds like a description straight from science fiction. And if these are our enemies, how on earth do we fight them? We can't see them.

This is certainly beyond burning witches at the stake. For one thing, that would be "wrestling flesh and blood," which a witch is. We do *not* wrestle flesh and blood. In some countries, the corrupt government is the enemy of the people, and so is the corrupt police system. Does that make them the Christian's enemy? They are flesh and blood. So they are not the enemy.

We're told first to take care of ourselves and to "put on the whole armor of God" (Ephesians 6:13–18). Not just the items we think we need, but the whole armor, so that every possible weakness and vulnerability is covered. This is still all defensive. Only a fool would go into offensive action without being prepared with a defense in case the enemy is stronger than he bargained for.

Truth is what the loins (waist) are girded with. Readily accessible at all times: the place the sword is attached and where a gun is strapped. What is truth? The question of the ages, the one

Pilate asked Jesus at His crucifixion. Jesus had told His disciples, "I am the way, the truth, and the life."

The breastplate of righteousness. If you don't care what righteousness is and think living any way you please is just fine, then you haven't protected your vital organ, the heart, so you're an easy mark for the enemy.

Feet shod with the gospel of peace. Not the mouth—the feet! This means you're supposed to be active with this gospel of peace, living it and not just talking it. In war? Come on—how can you spread peace? If you don't think about it, and don't try to, you won't.

Above all, the shield of faith. Nothing else will protect like faith. It quenches the fiery darts of the wicked (that sounds worse than bullets). The only way to extinguish them is faith. Not a squirt gun. Not a firehose. This shield is probably the part of armor that is attacked the most. If your faith is weak, it won't do a good job protecting you. Hmm. Is this why I've been failing?

Basic is the helmet of salvation. The enemy does aim for an unprotected head. Last is the only aggressive weapon: the sword of the Spirit. Sounds spooky if you stop there, but the Bible clarifies it: "which is the Word of God" (Ephesians 6:17).

That sure explains why so few Christians are winning any battles. They don't know anything about the Word of God. They don't even know the books of the Bible or how to find a verse. They don't know what it teaches. It's just a big mystery.

Most Christians are just sitting ducks.

CHAPTER 15

Winning Side

Do you want to be on the winning side when the game of life is over? At a basketball game, who knows which side is going to win before the game is over? Each side has its own strengths and weaknesses, and unexpected things always happen. If one side starts out on top, it is no guarantee they'll stay on top to the finish. The greatest games have been when someone on the bottom suddenly bursts forth in victory at the end to win the game by a narrow margin.

If you waver back and forth, only standing on the side that looks like it is winning, you will not be a valuable player or a useful supporter of either team. You may not lose, but you definitely won't win.

The battle between good and evil is a complicated competition. Where the devil himself is "transformed as an angel of light," a single human's judgment is simply not sufficient to make such an eternal decision. There are big questions: Who can I trust? What is the truth?

You can trust that God will lead you if you put your trust in Him—win or lose. Those who stand with Him only when it looks like He's winning (politically correct, what everybody's doing, the fad) are not with Him at all.

Those who stand with Him when it looks like He's losing will get in on the celebration when the race of life is over.

CHAPTER 16

Idolatry

How long halt ye between two opinions? If the LORD
be God, follow him: but if Baal, then follow him.
And the people answered him not a word.
—1 Kings 18:21

Many second-generation Christians today are in this same
position as the children of Israel when Elijah (the prophet God
commanded the ravens to feed) challenged them in his day. Christ
said, "No man can serve two masters: for either he will hate the one
and love the other; or else he will hold to one and despise the other.
Ye cannot serve God and mammon" (Matthew 6:24)

As the younger generation departs from church, is it the fault of
the older generation for scaring them away? Or are they responsible
for their own choice? The history of Israel, as recorded in the Bible,
is full of accounts of Israel departing from their God to serve the
gods of the nations around them. Those who stayed true to their
God were usually the remnant, the minority.

What is the idolatry of today that pulls people away from God?
One sixth-grade girl in my Sunday school class held up her iPhone
at this question. Everywhere you go, everywhere you look, people
of all ages are gazing at their little black boxes for whatever reason.

Colossians 3:5 refers to "covetousness which is idolatry." Who
is not bitten by this bug, desiring things we do not have? These
desired things are usually material and physical, but they could

also be circumstantial: desiring different circumstances in our life than what has been allotted to us. "Why did I get stuck with these problems? If I had been dealt George or Mary's hand of cards, I could deal with it, but this is a rotten hand I've been dealt." It's like the old folk song made famous by Kenny Rogers:

> You got to know when to hold 'em, know when
> to fold 'em, know when to walk away, and know
> when to run ... what to throw away, what to
> keep ... when the dealing's done.

We're stuck with the cards we're dealt in this game of life, and it's what we do with what we're dealt that makes all the difference. This is a truth witnessed both in Kenny Rogers's song and in Jesus's parable of the Master delivering different amounts of talents to his servants and leaving them to see what they would accomplish (Matthew 25:14–30).

> This is a rebellious people, lying children, children
> who will not hear the law of the LORD. (Isaiah 30:9)

Amazing how a book written by Jews about the Jews and their God should also be such a careful record of the many times they turned from their God to the idols of the people around them. What could be a better record of the holiness, justice, and mercy of that great God in His dealings with those people He called His own?

Today, the whole world—even the element that considers itself Christian—is almost totally in that position of rebellion that Israel has been in so often. They are rejecting the truth of the Word of God and going after the idols around them.

CHAPTER 17

Awe of Creator's Handwork

A Killdeer hunkered down over her eggs on the grass. A few starlings kept up the neighborhood patrol. I'm hearing other birds I can't see: such pleasant background music for a beautiful day. The House Sparrow just zipped by. She was probably going to her nest over my head, and then she changed her mind when she saw the enemy (me). Two mockingbirds are chasing each other across the parking lot.

Do those little black moths know where they are and where they are going? As they flutter around in the grass like flower petals in the wind, then suddenly take off with purpose, how do they know what they are doing? How do their little brains know where to go and what to do? If they aren't trained by parents, or taught from circumstances, where does their knowledge to exist long enough to reproduce or become the meal of another creature come from?

This is what I love about nature: while relaxing in serenity, beauty, and constant entertainment and celebration of life, there is just no end to the questions and awe at the handwork of a Creator who allows us to know Him through His handwork and His Word. And the observer doesn't need answers to his questions to enjoy these mysteries. Somehow, as questions build up, within and between them, sparks of understanding appear.

CHAPTER 18

Free as a Bird

The old adage "free as a bird" comes to mind when we don't want to be tied to responsibilities. But what an inappropriate phrase when all of the bird's life is spent "on alert" for predators. Of course, when they are in a flock (safety in numbers, important to remember) they may forage on the ground with heads down, but there are birds stationed at various points who seem to be "guards." At their signal, the flock rises together and circles before either returning or taking off. The threat may be only imagined, but pity the poor bird that doesn't heed it when it's real. That's how the hawk just got his meal.

What hawks are around believers, ready to pounce on some innocent who does not heed or hear warnings? In this culture, the dangers are everywhere: school, church, next door, and especially in our own homes (TV, computers, iPhones, etc.) This hawk could be someone we love, someone we hate, or someone we never knew.

The unseen hawk is ready to pounce on us in the place we feel happiest and safest, but the hawk that gets you may be different than the one eyeing me. Stay alert!

CHAPTER 19

The Enemy

One morning, as I settled into a good bird-watching spot, the birds seemed to be staying out of sight. I knew they were there. I could hear them. I decided to patiently wait, and I let my mind wander (something it does quite well).

My eye caught a movement, and I focused. A cat! Right by the vernal pool fence. I resisted the urge to jump up and chase it away. No bird has a complete education unless he's learned to deal with that sly four-footed predator lurking in the very grass that holds the bird's meal.

The bird has an advantage over this predator: wings! Though I've seen enough cats catch enough birds to know that advantage doesn't always help. This time it did, this little bird was alert. He escaped.

On the college patio, not far from the drama I had just witnessed, a small group of college students was praying. Who prowls around these young people (or anyone) looking for an unsuspecting moment to pounce? The devil goes about "as a roaring lion seeking whom he may devour" (1 Peter 5:8). If a lion were prowling around the campus, I don't think they'd be sitting there so peacefully. Look behind you! Is he there? Be alert, as birds are.

In a world where everyone calls everyone else a liar, from the government down to the preschool, with broken families all around, and clergymen and teachers molesting children, how do we teach our children whom to trust?

In the racist conflicts springing up lately, many are crying, "Don't let hate win!" With hatred such a cruel, strong bully, how can you stop it?

Christ said in Matthew 5: "Love your enemies." When Judas came to betray Him, Jesus called him "friend" (Matthew 26:50). God has a purpose in these enemies and betrayers beyond what is obvious in that moment.

Those who buck at "turning the other cheek" or at loving their enemies are like spectators watching a fistfight. They want victory here and now. They want to win the battle, but they forget you can win a battle and lose a war. Christ won the battle of the ages with one seeming defeat.

God's eye is on the whole picture (that we can't see) and not just one incident. That incident is part of a larger picture, and those who trust Him when it doesn't make human sense will have the satisfaction of being on the winning team. Though scripture reveals the outcome, God isn't revealing all the "plays." That's where we have to trust Him and obey, like a basketball player obeys his coach.

"Love your neighbor" was one of the Ten Commandments to the Jews. Jesus said to His followers: "Love your enemies." Plural—a lot more than one neighbor. No one had ever said anything like that before. As a mother, I sure wouldn't want to tell my children to love their enemies. I'd tell them to figure out who they are and run!

Jesus didn't run. With His death, He conquered sin and death.

Romans 12 talks about making our bodies a "living sacrifice." Not the same thing as being a martyr or a suicide bomber who dies. Our sacrifice is in our living and not in our death.

The end of the chapter says, "If your enemy hungers, feed him."

So, who is our enemy? The answer is different for each of us, and it is also different at different times of our life.

We don't flee. We love.

CHAPTER 20

Figuring My Limits

The carcass of a delicate beetle-like creature was at my feet. The distinct white lines on its back made it look like a chocolate truffle. I poked it with a stick. When it didn't move, I figured it was safe to pick it up. Delicate and paper like, it looked like its head was gone. Did its mate eat it, like the praying mantis?

Because this dead bug crossed my path (so to speak), I will think on it and marvel at its wonder, but I cannot allow this to cause me to choose a new path for my life: getting bug books and insect field books, and crawl on the ground searching new realms. No, I must stick to my bird books and the sky. Though I appreciate this awesome world at my feet, how will I ever get the bird world mastered if I try to do too much?

Now I can more appreciate the God who sees each sparrow fall, who numbers the hairs on each of our heads, as I see my limits and remember how unlimited He is.

CHAPTER 21

Designed

Remember that God designed you! He designed everybody who ever lived (even for a moment), is now living, or will ever live. Each creation has a part of the Creator, for humans were made in the image of God. Are we all just different chips off an infinite block? Maybe. Because we humans are limited and not infinite, we can only know God from each of our limited perspectives.

We, though in His image, have been corrupted. A beautiful bride's dress can show its original beauty even though a bucket of mud has been thrown on it, yet the original beauty is not noticed because of the spots. People don't say, "What a beautiful dress." Instead, they say, "Oh my! What happened?"

As we rub shoulders with people in the world around us, we are all covered with different amounts of mud, which sometimes stinks. We need to remember: under every mud-covered figure is an image of God. We can look for this, even if that person has wallowed in mud so long that no one has any idea there is any image of God within them. As we seek His image in others, and appreciate and love them, we can point them to the God who designed them, and to the Fountain He provided for their cleansing.

Those of us who see a clean white garment on ourselves are forgetting something. There is still our backside where mud may be splashed, and we can't see it. But others do. That's how we earn the label "hypocrite," and why we need fellow Christians to help us as we help them.

The devil, too, sees this image of God and is jealous. He was originally created perfect, but not "in the image of God." That's why he wants to destroy humankind. He uses war, drugs, addiction, attractive sin, and temptation to pull down this creature that God made in His image and died for.

CHAPTER 22

Unique Insignificance

Gazing out on a quiet vernal pool, I am distracted by a lone duck. Just to confirm that it is only a Mallard, and I need to think of it no more, I pull out my binocs and examine it closely. I don't recognize it! If it had been with a flock of Mallards, I'd never have paid attention. But since it was alone, I was forced to notice.

As I considered this unimportant duck, and appreciated its unique qualities, so the Lord wants me to take note of some "insignificant" person crossing my path. I took note of the bird's unique characteristics, so when I pulled my bird handbook out, I'd know what to look for. Later, with handbook, I narrowed it down to either a Redhead or Common Goldeneye—ducks I don't often see.

"Who is it that maketh thee to differ?" (1 Corinthians 4:7) refers to more than just physical characteristics. Differences in personalities and how our minds work also fit in this category of God's designing of unique creatures. Debating our different views with each other and trying to win others to our view is fine, as long as we remember that understanding comes from God—not our great learning.

We've each got our own blind spots, and that's why we need each other. We can live in harmony, even when we disagree, when we remember this. It is God who has made us different in mind *and* body.

CHAPTER 23

Camouflaged Christians

Just as the birds make you think they are gone because they are silent and camouflaged in their roosting places, so it seems that Christians are gone because they are silent and blend in well with the culture around them. Two Acorn Woodpeckers are crawling like beetles up the side of a telephone pole and then peeking over the edge at the top. If I hadn't known they always hung out there, I'd never have spotted them. Quiet, not even pecking or riveting, just looking like bolts on the telephone pole.

If Christians all disappeared (whether death, Rapture, or holocaust) would the world sense an emptiness when they are gone as a bird-watcher notices the emptiness when birds are not there? Or would everyone just go about their lives, never sensing any change? Do Christians today live lives so insignificant that no one will notice when they are gone? Another problem, contrary to being too much like the culture, could be that Christians have separated themselves so much from the culture (private schools, homeschooling) that the world never sees them.

Let us hope we sing as the birds, whether warbler or duck, so when that song is gone, the world will notice the silence.

CHAPTER 24

What Someone Else Thinks

What someone else thinks of you is out of your control and none of your business. That being said, what certain other people think of you may seem to make a difference in how your life goes. Does your boss value you or think you're worthless? Will this teacher's grade determine your academic fate? A partner wants to cut off relations with you because of what they believe you've done. These are more serious issues than some idle-minded gossip's rantings.

That being said, the thoughts of other people are still beyond your control. Manipulation is one thing—some people use it honestly, and some use it dishonestly—but manipulation is not control. "The king's heart is in the hand of the LORD: He turneth it whithersever He will" (Proverbs 21:1). The one truly in control is God.

Job's friends didn't think too highly of him, but God had His purpose in their thinking their erroneous thoughts (which each had a grain of truth in them, by the way). In the end, Job was lauded, and they were put down. But that was not until after Job had gone through a painful series of experiences.

We all want to be thought well of. Let's bear in mind, though, that the greatest man of all, Jesus Himself, was cursed, spoken ill of, and crucified. Whenever you hear someone curse, you can remember what He did for you and His great mercy for not striking the curser dead. God was in control of every thought and had His purpose in it.

While these hours of the Crucifixion were being experienced, how could anyone then know what it all meant? Looking back, we know. We have the written record in God's Word. But at that time, Christ's followers were stumbling in the dark, experiencing a horrible nightmare.

So it is with our lives, and why we can trust the Master Planner and not fear the fickle words of humans. Things may look bad, but God is in control, and we've put our trust in this God who created the universe.

CHAPTER 25

Consider the Ravens

Jesus said, "Consider the ravens." He didn't say, "Marvel how the raven takes care of himself." Instead, He pointed out how He provided for it. This was an object lesson from nature to illustrate a truth to His people: that He will provide. The skeptic will point to the bird that falls and becomes the meal of some predator and scoff that a loving God would do this. But that only illustrates another truth that is more difficult to understand. The time of one of His creatures was up (we know He sees the sparrow fall), and a meal was provided for another creature.

These ravens, "who neither sow nor reap," yet God provides for them, are in contrast with the ant, whom the sluggard is told "to go to the ant ... consider her ways and be wise; which having no guide, overseer or ruler, provideth her meat in the summer, and gathereth her food in the harvest" (Proverbs 6:6–8).

So, which is to be our example: the industrious ant or the unemployed raven? Obviously both, at different times. Once we've learned to work, like the ant, we need to quit depending on ourselves (if we are following Jesus) and learn to trust Him to provide as He leads us.

The young man who thinks his parents will provide for him, thus gives up on job searching, needs to "go to the ant." But the one following Jesus, who might have to give up a more secure income in order to minister for the Lord and reach the lost is the one who needs to "consider the raven."

CHAPTER 26

Nothing to Wear

"Do not worry ... what you will put on." Is that not what consumes a woman's mind so much of the time? Not so much that she has nothing to wear, but that, with a closet full of clothes, she has nothing to wear that suits that particular moment, event, or mood. Also, in considering that closet of clothes with no room to add more, what shall be tossed? Where will it go? What shall be replaced? From where? Highest-quality shop or thrift store? All time-consuming considerations. Life was much simpler when clothes were worn until they wore out and then became rags.

Back when I had less money, life was much simpler. Trusting the Lord to provide what to wear was one thing then. Now that I can go out and select what I want, there are so many more decisions and considerations. It does make me envy the birds. They don't have to decide what to wear as they start each day.

When Jesus told us not to worry about what to wear, He was telling the rich and poor alike, for each worried in a different way.

His instructions didn't stop with telling them what *not* to worry about. He went on with what *to* be concerned with: "Seek ye first the kingdom of God and his righteousness ... do not worry about tomorrow" (Matthew 6:25–34).

CHAPTER 27

Troubled Waters Alone

As we try to follow the Lord, we sometimes have to pass through troubled waters alone. We have to leave behind someone we expected to be with us, going on to make decisions and navigate life without their input.

We may have to leave our children to struggle with God for themselves, as Jacob did. As we did. We cannot give them the faith that is a gift from God alone (Ephesians 2:8–9). We can only pray they seek a personal faith for themselves. As we pray for those who have rejected the faith we seek to give them, we can reach out a helping hand to someone whose faith may be faltering, who seeks just the help we can give them at that moment.

Yes, we can trust the almighty omniscient God and Father to meet the needs of all His children at just the right time, just the right place, through just the right means. Both before and after our children were ours, they were God's. After we've done what we can, we must leave them to Him. He is the Author of their life—not us. We are the earthly parents or teachers.

CHAPTER 28

Annoying Birds

Among annoying birds, I'm sure the mockingbird is a contender for first place. Since I sat on this bench, expecting to enjoy a quiet morning observing the gentle birds, he has not shut up or turned down his volume. Because he made so much noise, I almost didn't notice the flock of Bushtits that flitted around in the oak tree for several minutes longer than their usual quick flash through.

I'm sure the mockingbird has his purpose—even though it conflicts with mine at the moment. Is his voice letting the other birds know it is safe? Maybe that's why the Bushtits stayed longer in the oak. I've seen him make a fuss over a hawk and play a part in the small bird posse as they chase a hawk from their territory.

So it is among a group of Christians. The one whose constant chirping may annoy others is the very source of comfort to someone else at some time. God uses each of His children in the lives of others in different ways at different times. We can appreciate our God more as we observe and appreciate the differences He has designed in each of His children. Others will appreciate us more if we appreciate them.

Puzzle Pieces of Life: Why Don't We All Believe the Same Thing?

Who loves putting a puzzle together? Life is like a box of puzzle pieces that each tries to sort and arrange for himself or herself. Everyone is given a different box in this puzzle entitled "Life." Some of the pieces are the same in each box, and some are different. No picture comes with this box, though many claim they have figured out or know what it is going to be.

When the theology of two godly people is different, it begins a controversy. Both can't be right. Even though both use particular puzzle pieces straight from scripture to back up their picture claims, they use different scriptures for some reason and rule out others for another reason ("Because the audience is Old Testament Jews—not New Testament church!"). Some descend into the finer points of translation of Hebrew or Greek, splitting hairs to make their theological points.

God doesn't give everyone the same understanding. That's why one's concept of the same scripture is different from another's. The scripture comes from Him, and the understanding comes from Him. Each person is responsible for what God has given them, and cannot judge their brother or sister for not seeing things their way, for understanding does not come from intelligence or learning, but from God (Luke 24:45). The uniqueness of each individual is God's design, not their own choosing. "For who makes you differ from another? And what do you have that you did not receive?" (1 Corinthians 4:7).

What is the puzzle you are grappling with? There is no end of issues to take sides on. Ask any librarian who must help people on both sides of an issue find material to prove their point. From free will and election to universalism and limited atonement, each pulls out his Bible to prove his point. They have many of the same puzzle pieces, but put them in different places, and in the gaps where no piece is, they have drawn their own lines.

Why would God write such a book that kept people grappling over it for thousands of years? If they'd agreed, they'd probably have stopped searching. How could we appreciate our infinite, omniscient, almighty God if He didn't continue to challenge us to keep reaching beyond our comfort zone of understanding? Wake up.

And watch. Someone you once thought was on a different side of an issue you may meet on a different mountain in this same range. The issue was bigger than both thought it was.

Obviously God allows misunderstanding. The disciples thought they chose Christ: "We have found the Messiah" (John 1:41). Later, Christ says, "Ye have not chosen me but I have chosen you" (John 15:16).

In the meantime, we'll each keep working with the pieces God has given us. We can hoard our findings or share them. As we hoard, we continue in the darkness of our own misunderstanding. But as we share, it opens us up to the spotlights of critics. What better way to stretch our minds and see more clearly?

The picture is bigger than anyone thought it was.

CHAPTER 30

Escape: Good or Bad?

Everyone needs an escape now and then, to get away from the continual pressures of life that are a struggle day after day and simply don't go away.

As a young housewife with a growing family, one of my escapes from the pressure of a chaotic, messy household was in the quiet, orderly aisles of the supermarket. Logic, order, a place for everything, and everything in its place. But eventually I got all the groceries and had to go back to the never-ending battle and make do with whatever order I could manage.

Maybe "escape" is why I took an interest in birds. I could observe them, appreciate their beauty, identify them, and enjoy their diversity and harmony, but I didn't have to take care of them! They took care of themselves. When I'd had enough, I could put away my binoculars and go back to my business.

Wilderness escapes seem so ideal. That's why camping is popular. Even Jesus retreated to the wilderness after the pressure of the multitude. Refreshed, He went back to face the multitude again.

Escapes take many forms. Some people resort to drugs or alcohol. Technology is a vice for others. Are escapes good or bad?

A good escape is a look away from the normal, everyday world and its problems. It refreshes, refocuses, and helps one come back and face the usual with new appreciation and perspective.

The escape one person chooses can be a common bond with another person who takes an interest in the same things (like bird-watching, hiking, camping). Or it can be a wall, if no one shares the interest with you or appreciates your stories.

Bird-watching usually helps me sort out life and deal with problems, providing needed meditation time. But if I spend too much time with it, and use it to escape my problems, it has defeated my purpose of refreshment and is no longer a good thing. Balance must be kept.

CHAPTER 31

Faith: Tossing Mountains

Some have the faith that perceives God as a tool in their hand, rather than the faith of the one who sees himself as a tool in God's hand. The weaker prayer is that God does this or that in this particular way at this particular time. Yes, God does honor weak faith, for Jesus even said that all it took was faith as the grain of a mustard seed to cast a mountain into the sea.

But just how weak is mustard seed faith? Have you ever seen a mountain cast into the sea?

Back in May 1980, I was talking about faith to an older man in a park in Tacoma, Washington. He was scornful of faith in something he could not see, but he really laughed at the idea that it only took faith the size of a mustard seed to cast a mountain into the sea. Who had ever seen anything like that?

Just two days later, on May 18, 1980, Mount Saint Helens erupted. Some friends and I hopped in a car and saw it live from a spot as close to it as the highway patrol allowed us to get. Soon, all the world would see how a mountain was picked up, dropped into the Toutle River, carried to the Columbia River, and sent out to the Pacific Ocean.

That's the picture of mustard seed faith. Nothing to scoff at!

Was Christ telling His followers to go tossing mountains around? He spoke so often in parables—maybe this was another one. What could be a bigger mountain than some issue we face in our lives or some stubborn person who refuses to cooperate with us?

The most awesome thing about watching Saint Helens blow was seeing that tremendous unstoppable power released in billow after billow from a previously quiet, still mountain. According to the US Geological Survey, it released "24 megatons of thermal energy … this is the equivalent to 1,600 times the size of the atomic bomb dropped on Hiroshima."

Jesus's habit was not to dismiss issues with quick answers but to raise more questions so people would think more. Was He telling the disciples to move mountains if He had never done it?

Zechariah spoke of a mountain that would become a plane:

> Not by might nor by power, but by My Spirit, says
> the LORD of hosts. Who are you, O great mountain.
> (Zechariah 4:6–7)

There are several other kinds of faith referred to in scripture. There's the mustard tree that has more than just the potential of the seed but serves people and gives rest to the fowls of the air. There's faith like the "great cloud of witnesses" in Hebrews 11 that subdued kingdoms, etc.

Lest anyone get puffed up about their faith, we are reminded in Ephesians 2:8–9 that we are saved by grace through faith—and that faith is a gift of God.

CHAPTER 32

Disappointed Expectations of Parents

Do birds have expectations, either for themselves or their offspring, as people do? Most are protective of their eggs and nestlings, but when they are out of the nest and finding their own food, they are on their own. Birds only worry about the here and now, the next meal. That's why they are a lesson to us to trust God to provide. But He didn't tell us to copy birds all the time in every way. The scripture tells us to "train up a child in the way he should go." Maybe some birds do train their young (I'll have to look into that), but I just haven't observed it among the birds here at the vernal pool. The book of Job (Job 39:13–15) speaks of the ostrich who lays her eggs in the dust and forgets about them. That does describe a lot of parents in our world today.

There is the pain of a parent whose child has been involved in crime—even murder. The first murder in the Bible was a brother killing a brother. There was no quick, easy solution. There was a punishment for the crime, and the grieving parents had to deal with disappointed expectations for their first son and the loss of their second son. This was the first human death experienced.

As parents, we imagine our children will be everything we hope them to be. Then time passes. Life and its afflictions roll over them, and they don't pass every test. In the fog of life, a different image is emerging than what we thought was there. Failing perceptions and disappointed expectations is what we must deal with on both sides: both parent and child of each other. This is what we should lay before the Lord and leave there.

The role of the parent in the child's life is almost done. Now they must walk their own road of life independent of their parent. If they choose the broad way rather than the narrow, the parent can only pray they will encounter God and make the right choice before it is too late.

The parent's heart breaks as the child becomes almost a stranger in a world getting crazier every day. Yet God is in control—not the parent. He knows what He is doing, and He will be glorified in the outcome. Not the parent. A large dose of faith is needed here.

If all families were strong and stable, who would need God? As the families begin to crack and crumble, whoever calls on the name of the Lord shall be saved. Not those who have a good pedigree and a fine family. It is "whosoever believeth" that has everlasting life, not whosoever is born into some family and baptized.

If I do what I do because I love the Lord, why should I expect my children to make those choices because that was how I "trained" them? The parent sometimes has the false notion that the child is a little copy of himself or herself and will do what the parent did even better since the parent trained, equipped, and educated them. We failed to take into account that they have their own minds and process knowledge in different ways than we do. Their eyes see the same thing we do in different ways, and their ears follow a different drummer.

We watch our children disappearing on a trail of life different than the one we have trod. They face enemies different than the ones we have faced. They embrace as friends what we would have considered enemies. And if we speak against these friends, we become as an enemy to them.

We watch them on this trail they have chosen, hoping they will learn the hard way through their own mistakes. We tried to teach them through our mistakes, but that didn't work.

They seem like the people Jeremiah had to minister to, who rejected God's way, wanted only their own way, and refused to listen to the prophet who warned them that God would judge them for their disobedience. A mother's protection is no help here. They must encounter God for themselves, and the parent fears that encounter will not be good since they have ignored what God says.

Parents do not know their heart, and they can only judge from outward appearances. All they can do is pray and leave them in God's hands: "It is a fearful thing to fall into the hands of the living God" (Hebrews 10:31).

CHAPTER 33

Are Birds Racist?

Many birds, such as the Canada Geese, seem to find safety and strength as they stick together in their own flocks. They sometimes allow other species of water birds, such as Mallards or Yellowlegs, to dip around in the water with them.

Foraging on the ground, one will often see Brewer's Blackbirds or Brown-headed Cowbirds among starlings. So, they don't seem racist.

Then there are those who forage on their own, not even seeking a flock of their own kind. Even these will band together with birds of other species to chase away a common foe: the hawk.

Is finding a common foe the secret to overcoming racism?

Thirty years ago, I was part of a church by a military base. This was an "integrated" church without necessarily intending to be. Many of the members had served the military in various places around—the world from Germany to Korea—and all had stories to swap with each other. Their common purpose was protecting the United States. Don't know who the foe was, but they were ready if one should appear.

God has unusual ways of revealing His light in our darkening world. A white boy in Charleston, South Carolina, went to a black church, and after sitting with them for an hour, pulled out a gun and killed nine of them. With the other race-related riots and protests in our country at this time (June 2015), what will the reaction to this be?

The world was dumbfounded as families of the murdered people spoke the words of forgiveness amidst their pain and sorrow: "We're not going to let hate win." Instead of the riots and violence that have been exploding between blacks and whites, the news showed black and white coming together, all comforting this bereaved community and families at this awful time.

Hate didn't win here.

CHAPTER 34

Patience in Waiting for Birds and Blessings

Another day when not a bird is in sight. If I pull out my notebook and start writing, maybe I will fool them, they'll think I'm not watching, and then come out to tease me. I take pen to paper. My eye catches a movement in the top of a tree. A Yellow-rumped Warbler! No, two—three are bouncing around, but quietly. I turn my eyes back to my notebook to describe them, and I begin to hear other birds: the croak of an Acorn Woodpecker and the pitiful squeak of a starling.

Another bird twitters from the tree right in front of me, but I can't see it. These once-naked twigs have sprouted glorious, tender green leaves. Up at the top, I see a Lark Sparrow framed by a halo of these leaves, lifting his beak to sing to the sky, to the God who composed his song. Now he's gone to another spot, and I can't see him. But I can still hear his song, like a memory trailing behind.

In a sad, dreary world, these bright little spots of color and song remind us there is hope from the God of all consolation.

CHAPTER 35

Did I Tell You about My New Binoculars?

These new powerful binoculars sure change my perspective on life! Suddenly, the old, boring landscape is bouncing with life. The bark on a distant tree, each leaf in detail, not just a green hat stuck on a gray stump. A hundred yards away, I can tell the Killdeer from the Yellowlegs (probably a Lesser Yellowlegs since it's close to the size of the Killdeer). Yesterday, after I bought the binoculars, I hurried back to the vernal pool to see what I could see.

The Great Egret (whom I've nicknamed "the Crabby Bachelor" because he chases away every other egret that comes to the pool) was sharing space in the middle on a slight rise with a Great Blue Heron. With my old binocs, earlier in the day, I'd observed them both as fuzzy shapes (but not so fuzzy that I couldn't identify them) as they stood, side by side in the water at the north side of the pool. Through the day, as I looked out the library window, I saw them each making their way south on different sides, eventually meeting again, and finally side by side in the middle where everyone could see them, like a bride and groom surrounded by a lively party.

I have great expectations for these new binoculars. Maybe to see the Wilson's Snipe again, a shy little bird that huddles in the grass. I'd never have noticed if a student hadn't asked, "What's that bird by the fencepost?" In every step of life, we profit from the observations of others. Otherwise, we might never see what is right in front of our eyes.

So, in writing observations of life, the writer bares his soul to put down what he perceives so the reader can examine and decide if this fits with his own observations. Does it help him understand—or is it not worth wasting his time with? This communication needs to go both ways, the reader responding to the writer and sharing his thoughts, then the understanding of both can be developed.

CHAPTER 36

Let Your Light Shine

Let your light so shine before men, that they may see your
good works and glorify your Father which is in heaven.
—Matthew 5:16

So, as I am tucked away in the library, doing those necessary,
behind-the-scenes tasks that no one sees or appreciates, my light
is shining before no one. When I'm bird-watching, also a task for a
loner, my light only shines before the birds, which certainly don't
care.

But it is in these alone times that my thoughts develop, like a
hatchling inside an egg. Yes, even when my mind is wrestling with
work problems, my mind breaks from these obligations like the
hatchling from its shell, and suddenly, I get an idea I want to write
about. Usually I can take time to write down the idea in order to
come back and develop it at an appropriate time.

When it's finally written, that's when the light is shining before
men, not just hidden under my bushel.

CHAPTER 37

Some Birds Care—Some Birds Don't Care

Do birds fret about their young, whether they will learn to take care of themselves, find food, and watch for predators? Some don't. The Bible speaks of the ostrich, who God has deprived of wisdom, which lays her egg in the dust and forgets about it as she flutters here and there. Yet somehow, the young ostrich must make it. Otherwise, ostriches would have gone extinct. Some human mothers are like that too, forgetting their offspring as they flutter here and there, consumed with their own drama.

Other birds hover protectively around their young constantly. Yesterday, I watched a female Mallard with seven little ducklings (may have been more, may have been less, but they didn't stop moving as they wiggled and splashed around their mother, so I couldn't be sure of the count). Are they learning from their mother how to swim and how to find food in water or on land? Are these innate behaviors? Will a duckling deprived of its mother simply become fresh meat for a predator—or does it have good chance to survive? Right now, I'm stockpiling questions quicker than I can find answers.

I saw two female Lesser Goldfinches flying from a campus tree to the parking lot fountain, back to the tree, then back to the fountain, with one never letting up her scolding chatter and the other seeming to try to escape it. Was I witnessing a mother trying to teach her daughter how to get along in this dangerous world, while the daughter wanted no part of it? Questions, questions.

That's all my observations bring me. For everything I find out now, there is far more I don't know.

The Killdeer lays her eggs on the ground in sticks and leaves. But she stays close by, using her broken wing trick if a predator should appear. One of the college students thought a little bird tried to attack him as he shuffled through the leaves. "Ah," I said. "You must have been near the Killdeer's nest!

And just as some birds care for their young, and others do not (or so it seems), so there are human mothers who care for their young, while others don't (or so it seems). The uncared-for bird can claim the promise that God sees even the sparrow fall. The human can claim Psalm 27:10: "When my father and mother forsake me, then the LORD will take me up."

There are a lot of forsaken people in this world today, from aborted babies to foster care and abused children to the homeless who wander from place to place. Human, caring mothers are just a temporary thing, especially in times of war. So many countries are now facing war, and will America also, with North Korea making foolish threats? Scripture says, "Vain is the help of man." Only God can save us from impossible situations, both physically with this life and eternally with our souls.

CHAPTER 38

Job's Refocus

The book of Job certainly deals with the basics of human life and suffering, asking more questions (seemingly) than it answers. Job's three friends came to console him in the wake of losing his children, his wealth, and his health—just like people today with their pathetic attempts to give advice to someone who is suffering. "Miserable comforters are ye all," says Job. After Job and his friends are finally through talking, God speaks.

What He doesn't tell Job (at least at first): He had pointed Job out to the devil and boasted about him! "Hast thou considered my servant Job?" The devil is scornful of Job's righteousness: "Sure, you've put a hedge around him! Take those things away, and he will curse you." So, the Lord allows the devil to take all these things (listed in the first two chapters of Job).

Job finally does some complaining and wishes he'd never been born. But of God, he says, "Though he slay me, yet will I trust him."

As well as having a God he trusts so completely, Job has a hope that no one else has yet expressed:

> For I know that my redeemer liveth, and that he shall stand at the latter day upon the earth. And after my skin worms destroy this body, yet in my flesh I shall see God, whom I shall see for myself. (Job 19:25–27)

Much in Job is hard to understand because of the distance of time and culture, but there's no mistaking that hope. It should have brought his friends up short, but they just carried on their criticisms.

What God *does* tell Job doesn't seem to have any bearing on his situation. He doesn't have sympathy or pity, but he proceeds to put Job in his place: "Who is this who darkens counsel by words without knowledge?" (Job 38:2).

He reminds Job of the immensity of his God. "Where were you when I laid the foundation of the earth? Tell me if you have understanding."

God describes all kinds of amazing things in His creation: "God thundereth marvelously with his voice; great things doeth he which we cannot comprehend" (Job 37:5).

At this point, I want to start researching and reading all I can find about the animals God reminded Job about. He was exalting His own creation to Job, showing that these creatures were important and worthy of Job's notice. These were part of God's big picture, of which Job was also a part.

We are, too often, like Job, getting wrapped in our own pity party, and needing to be reminded, like Job, of the awesome creation around us that we are a small part of.

Job repented (Job 42:6), and "the LORD blessed the latter end of Job more than his beginning" (Job 42:12).

CHAPTER 39

Crabby Bachelor Holds His Spot

Scripture tells us to learn from the animals, fowl, and fish (Job 12:7–8). We try. Isn't that how we got airplanes and submarines?

Yesterday, as the Crabby Bachelor dominated the vernal pool, I saw two other Great Egrets land in the pine tree southeast of the pool. At the same time, another Great Egret circled the pool and then slowly settled in the eucalyptus northwest of the pool. Every time I looked out a window for the next hour, all four held their positions.

Eventually, when I looked, only the Crabby Bachelor remained in his central spot. The two trees were empty. He had shared the pool with the Great Blue Heron about a week ago—but not with his own kind.

This is just an observation recorded. No meditations at this time. But maybe the drama will go on.

CHAPTER 40

What God Didn't Tell Us

How can we mortals, whose lives are totally governed by space and time, comprehend when "time shall be no more"? What will it be like? Will none of this earth's scientific laws apply, like gravity and physics? Those who go into outer space experience strange things, like weightlessness, away from gravity and air.

Obviously, God didn't mean for us to occupy ourselves continually with thoughts on the hereafter, for His Word was given (spoken before written) that man might know how to best make use of himself and the resources God gave him on earth in the present. Dealing with sin is the major problem, for this is what messes life up. The man who acknowledges the enemy (sin) as stronger than he is, can "put on the whole armor of God" and be prepared to "fight against the wiles of the devil."

Many of those missing puzzle pieces of life may be revealed to us in that state of "time no more." If not, we'll certainly be content to live with such knowledge as He wills us to have, no longer lusting for the tree of the knowledge of good and evil.

For the present, how are we to live? With the resources God has given us. What are they? As in the parable of the master handing out talents, he has given different amounts to each servant, and each is responsible for what he is given. Little or much. The same can apply to those who know theology up and down, the Bible back and forth, and those who don't even know the Bible at all.

Every minute of life is a lesson from and communication with

God. What do we do with that communication? Do we complain because we want what someone else has been given and not want what has been doled to us? Better to rejoice in what has been given us, make the fullest use of it we can, and ask God to open our eyes to what is before us that we are somehow blind and deaf to appreciating.

CHAPTER 41
Chorus Line Performance

I have commenced the quiet sitting and waiting time in my bird-watching ritual. I've just listed in my bird notebook eleven species that I've seen in thirty minutes, most on the vernal pool at the same time. Now, as I sit behind the library (about a hundred feet from the pool), I wait for the birds here to show themselves.

No sooner do I take up pen and turn my eyes from the trees but four Acorn Woodpeckers land around me: in the oak, on the ground, on the side of the building beside me. They keep moving. I hear starlings as well as the continual croak of an Acorn Woodpecker. I see an occasional flash of a distant wing, but it's suddenly pretty still. I may get a last-minute rush of birds, their little chorus line and variety entertainment right when I have to go in.

The longer I sit quietly in one spot, the more likely I am to get the show. Patience. One bird landed in the grass, but I can't see him now. How many more are there, just peeping out at me and I can't see them? A Western Bluebird was calmly observing me from the oak in front of me. How long has he been there?

My time is up. This wasn't as impressive a chorus line as I've seen other times. I can always look forward to seeing something better another time: both with birds and with life.

DRY SEASON

CHAPTER 12

GWFG

Everything looks as still as a painting, but my eye keeps seeking, savoring every texture of bark, every blade of several kinds of grass. Suddenly, there is a slight movement in this still life. In the grass and reeds at the northwest corner of the vernal pool, a long neck with a smudge of white around its beak sticks up. Then a second one pops up. Just two. Were these two Greater White-fronted Geese left behind from the flocks that migrated through in March? It's now May.

On May 5, I begin watching every day for those pink faces on the northwest side of the vernal pool (much dried up by now). Every day I see them until May 12. The "mosquito guys" are coming now (their name is more official than that, but I can't think of what it is)! As they go slogging through the vernal pool, spraying the chemical that is supposed to reduce the number of mosquitoes produced by the drying waters, the quiet still life comes alive!

Mama Mallard with her five growing ducklings clustered around her paddled off toward the south side, as did all the other Mallards. The two Greater White-fronted Geese began waddling to the east, but as the mosquito guys caught up with them, one flew off and the other waddled to the grass on the side. Was it lame? Had its partner stayed with it until this?

A large flock of Red-winged Blackbirds rose, some crisscrossing across the pool with the swallows (some Bank Swallows, for sure, and at least one Tree Swallow). The Great Egret was there and flew to the south side with the Mallards, as well as a Bufflehead and a couple of Northern Shovelers.

For about a week after this I still saw the two GWFG in the grasses on the north side. Then I saw them no more.

CHAPTER 43
Danger

As peaceful and serene as the landscape may be, and as much as it soothes my mind and gives me rest from the worries and troubles that bombard me daily, I'm still reminded that danger is not far away. The quiet is split by the cry of the Killdeer. Danger is near her nest, and she's letting everyone know as she flies off, seeking to distract this danger near her eggs.

Danger. Am I in any danger today? Not that I know of. But as Ephesians 6:12 reminds us: "We wrestle not against flesh and blood, but against principalities, powers, the rulers of the darkness of this world." These are definitely unseen enemies, and who can say when they will attack if you cannot see them?

Be alert—both physically and spiritually.

CHAPTER 11

God's Way

The grass withers, the flower fades, but the
word of our God stands forever.
—Isaiah 40:8

As the vernal pool dries with rising temperatures (we've had a week in the nineties), birdlife around here changes. There are still two female Mallards with their ducklings (where are the males?). One set is four "teenage" ducklings, while the other set looks like furry brown chicks, moving under and around their mother so quickly I can't count them. Off at the edge, I still see one Greater White-fronted Goose, probably the one that is lame. Was it left behind by its partner?

With my new binoculars, I now see insects and even spider webs laced across the grasses of the vernal pool like a sparkling diamond net as the sun rises. None of these could be seen by the eye alone—or even with my old binoculars. I'm in a superior position of judgment now!

As I watch the "grass wither" and the "flower fade," I realize that is God's way. It is only His Word that lasts forever. Some of His works, which were masterpieces, still wither and die. I will do my best with what I'm given to work with—even though it will wither and die.

CHAPTER 15

Man Looks to His Maker

What causes a man to look to his Maker? Certainly it is not when he prospers and all goes well with him. At such a time, he does not need his Maker. He only needs himself. Isaiah 17 describes a list of woes beginning: "The burden of Damascus ... it will be a ruinous heap ... forsaken ... In that day will a man look to his maker."

So it seems to be with each individual man. Until he hits rock bottom, until he sees his own efforts cannot save or lift him, he will not look up. Isaiah warns: "But the harvest will be a heap of ruins in the day of grief and desperate sorrow" (Isaiah 58:11).

Isaiah is so depressing to read, for right and left are the nations getting judgment for their sins. Then, in the middle of it, is the promise: "He will swallow up death in victory; and the LORD will wipe away tears from off all faces." The judgment of the nations, but the comfort is to "all faces" that the tears will be wiped from. What a day, what a hope!

Then the promise: "Behold, this is our God; we have waited for him and he will save us ... We will be glad and rejoice in his salvation" (Isaiah 25:9).

The warning: "The LORD cometh to punish the inhabitants of the earth for their iniquity" (Isaiah 26:21).

Until we know the punishment we deserve, how can we appreciate the grace and forgiveness offered to us?

CHAPTER 16
Watch. Wait. Now.

The vernal pool is certainly no pool in late May. It is a field of grass, reeds, and wildflowers, still green before all the moisture gets sucked from the earth by the unmerciful sun. As I scanned with my binoculars, I saw no sign of the Mallards or the one Greater White-fronted Goose. A few Cliff Swallows dived for bugs, and some smaller birds chased off two low-flying ravens. Do these predators find meals in stranded, helpless birds like that lame Greater White-fronted Goose? Yesterday I saw a hawk (smaller than the Red-tailed or Red-shouldered Hawk) dive into the grasses on the west bank. Did it stay there and finish some meal it snatched?

Watch and *wait* are two very appropriate words, both spiritually and in bird-watching. I'll bet these are two of the most used words in the Bible. "Wait on the Lord and he shall strengthen thine heart." "Watch ... for at an hour ye think not the Son of man cometh"

But in our current world, with technology outdating itself daily, the word is *now*! Quick! Instantly!

What the Bible says about *now*: "Behold, now is the day of salvation" (2 Corinthians 6:2).

CHAPTER 47

Judging Others

When we would judge those around us for their unbelief, hardness of heart, blindness to truth, disobedience, or just because they have a different opinion, we need to stop and follow the children of Israel through the wilderness, then the time of the judges and kings, and finally their exile and captivity. The history was recorded so that we might learn from their experiences, mistakes, and victories.

In Lamentations, we hear the mournful cries of Jews that echo through time, for what people have been more oppressed throughout the world and history than the Jews? In their cries from oppression are also the cries of other oppressed people: the slaves in American history or victims of war in Africa and Asia. Recorded are Jeremiah's lamentations. He speaks of God "like a flaming fire devouring all around, standing like an enemy" (Lamentations 2:3)

Any who have felt that God was their enemy could not have experienced it more than the Jews. How much can one people endure? Lamentations 3 pours out so much for one individual. In the midst of this horror, the light of hope dispels the darkness:

> Through the LORD's mercies we are not consumed,
> because His compassions fail not ... Great is your
> faithfulness ... the LORD is good to those who wait
> for Him. (Lamentations 3:21–26)

Do I rejoice in the Word of God as much as I rejoice in material riches (Psalm 119:14)?

Who will not whoop and holler when they win some unexpected jackpot? Even the woman in Jesus's parable who found her lost coin (Luke 15:9) rejoiced with her friends when she found it. There is nothing wrong with that, but do I rejoice as much in God's Word as I do in money? God does not give wealth to everyone, and He does not give the desire for His Word to everyone. So, if He gives me His Word, and gives me love for it, then indeed I am blessed.

There was a time when I read God's Word just because it was a habit. I even thought it was boring. Now, when I find something in it that meets a need, gives hope, answers a question, or spurs me on, I rejoice. I'm even thankful for the times when I thought it boring. I can be patient with those who think it boring since I once was there. Someday, their blind eyes will open to its treasure—as mine did.

CHAPTER 18

Prophets Depressing, But ...

Reading through the Bible prophets (Isaiah, Jeremiah, Ezekiel, etc.,) can be depressing. The thunder of God's wrath is falling on His people. They have been warned many times that this would be the consequences of their actions, but still they turn away from the true God to seek gods more pleasing to them among the false gods of the Gentiles.

Ezekiel is the prophet with the strangest visions and creatures like science fiction (competition for *Star Wars*). However, rays of hope flash in bleak spots:

> They that wait upon the LORD shall renew their strength. They shall mount up with wings as eagles, they shall run and not be weary, they shall walk and not faint. (Isaiah 40:3)

CHAPTER 49

Band Together: Identify the Enemy

When I arrived at the parking lot a drama was unfolding. The Western Kingbirds were making a fuss and circling over the weeping willow. Suddenly, a hawk emerged and headed for an oak with half a dozen of these little birds dive-bombing him. From there, he fled across the parking lot (still pursued) to the eucalyptus, then to the oaks across the dried-up vernal pool.

Lesson in that? Little ones can band together against a bully or predator.

What are the hawks in my life that someone else could help me with? Maybe some person looking for a weakness they can pounce on and cause my downfall? Or maybe my hawk is not a person to identify and confront, but some lust of my own: chocolate, television, gaming, or gossip. So, as the little birds in the drama— don't just flee the predator—attack him! Rally all your good habits like little birds: nibble a piece of celery, grab pen and paper, turn eyes to some spot in nature (even just a weed in the concrete crack), or quote some scripture. That way, the little birds (various insignificant good habits) can defeat the big bad one, which, like a predator, is often hidden and unnoticed.

CHAPTER 50

Getting Ready for the Enemy

Is the world any different today than it was yesterday? Sitting here behind the library, I see the same western foothills, the same skyline framed by oaks, and the same local birds darting about their business. Could there be war going on in this peaceful world before me?

Here is a lesson. The birds are not fooled by a peaceful seeming landscape. They know the threat is real even if they cannot see it. They live cautiously. One of their threats is that relative of the "roaring lion seeking whom he may devour" that is no threat to humans (the cat). Another is one of their own kind: a fellow bird. But predators and raptors have established their reputation, though they be birds.

Not all birds are cautious and careful, though. Some are like the Bufflehead, who had a great time splashing and diving until the eagle swooped down and snatched him. But even a little bird with careful habits has no defense against the quiet hawk observing it from a tree and swooping down at an unsuspecting moment to snatch him.

Even as I enjoy this serene landscape (no hawk in sight), I feel the evil oppression of the world around me, threatening me and those I love. Along with the fear that they may be targets of the enemy is the fear that they will be tools of the enemy. This is the time to remember that the apostle Paul had certainly been on the enemy's side, and God transformed him.

Churches are on the front line of the battle, and the wounded of both sides are here. The soldiers themselves are not always sure who is friend or foe. Jesus covered all bases when He told us to love our enemies.

If all birds cowered in their nests just because a predator might be near, no birds would survive. Survival involves risk and trust. The sweet little warbler certainly makes himself a target, but how quiet and sad the world would be without that song to lift the hearts of those who hear it.

To live in constant fear of the enemy and what he can do is to be in bondage to him. Ignoring the threat is not taking care of it either. To be able to look to the Lord—who has power over all things and is our Savior from any threat and danger—is an option I want to cling to. His strength is beyond any human achievement.

"Whom shall I fear?" is the issue in Psalm 27. This is the question of all questions, implying first of all that fear is a very real power. Something needs to be feared, but what?

"The LORD is my light and my salvation: whom shall I fear?" If we have this light, we need not fear all the dangers of darkness: shadows, pitfalls, lurking enemies, land mines, whatever. As well as being my *light*, the LORD is my *salvation*.

A savior and salvation are important when there is something to be saved from. What great dangers are of the darkness? What is invisible and more dangerous because we cannot see them?

God is selecting soldiers for His army. He's not choosing the fearless and strong. He's choosing those who trust Him as their light and salvation. He's choosing the foolish and weak (1 Corinthians 1:27–29)

As Psalm 27 reminds us: "Wait on the LORD." He will strengthen your heart, but you need to wait.

CHAPTER 51

Control

My life was planned clear till the end of summer, even to the very day before me, just who I would talk to, what I would find out, what I would take care of. All necessary steps for summer.

Who was to know I was to twist and stretch just a little too far, fall, and pull my left hip out of its socket? I screamed from the small bathroom floor, and my husband tried to help, but every touch or slightest move was another jolt of pain, another scream, and his only choice was to call the emergency room. Eventually, the sound of distant sirens arriving broke through the pain. Both paramedics and firemen were there, crawling into our little closet bathroom and trying to figure out how to get this old lady out to the ambulance.

A medic asked, "On a scale of one to ten, what is your pain level?"

I'd always prided myself in enduring pain, but today I answered, "Twenty!"

The pain did not lessen until long after I was at the hospital and finally knocked out with anesthesia.

From the hospital bed, I had a chance to think of my plans. I was missing all the people I looked forward to seeing all week long: the kids who came to the children's service at church, the adults I prayed for every day (and one by one seem to be slipping away), and various others for whatever reason. On Sunday, the Teen Challenge group was to give their testimonies! I was missing these accounts of young women who'd been freed from the bondage of addiction.

Finally, I was taken to the room where the procedure was to be done (was I already "out of it" by then?) My husband and Laura told me later about the x-ray machine that showed the bone moving as the physician twisted it back into place. Then I was wheeled back to a recovery room. Besides the medical team attending me, and my family watching, there were three paramedics-in-training observing things around the emergency room, observing this life they were learning to play a part in. I got to be an object lesson. I had a nice chat with them and got to be an encouragement to them in the goal they were pursuing.

Of course, the hand of God controlled all this. There is no way I could have known about or planned to play a role in the lives of these young men I'd never seen before and would probably never see again. But God designed the paths of all our lives, and He knew just when to intersect paths that would not otherwise cross in order to have an exchange that would be mutually beneficial, though unexpected.

So, while I cling tightly to this wheel I think is controlling my life, God is still in control and will even override my good plans when they cross His better plans.

Now, as I learn again how He is in control, I learn (more to my frustration) how I need to depend on other people for the simplest things. I cannot even put on my own socks. One foot has a sock half on that I got there by using a little stick with a hook on it, but I cannot bend or twist (such simple movements) in any way. That's how I got the hip out of its socket.

I sit helplessly, missing my morning walk. When will I get to do it again?

Even my library work will now be more limited since I can't lift boxes or stacks of books. Others will have to be my hands and feet. Sweetness and gratefulness are two things I'll have to work on.

Is that why the Lord let this happen to me?

CHAPTER 52

Concrete Walk

After my accident and several weeks of rest, I gradually began resuming my morning walking. It's now more modified than my usual trek around the blocks where my apartment is, where the only spot that isn't concrete or asphalt is the corner of one empty lot. I call it my "concrete walk." This is very much a city and not the nature of country, which I prefer.

Nature still "taints" everything—no matter how much humans have made things to try to stamp it out. A weed bursts out of the crack of the sidewalk. A small flock of finches (not sure which kind) takes off chattering in alarm as the noisy trucks of man arrive. Road workers are planning to repave the road today. Does technology of man win the war with nature? The pigeons flutter in circles in a flock together and then go back to their usual hangout on the sign of Home Depot. But they stay alert.

While I walked, a Scrub Jay was squawking and letting all the local birds know something new was approaching. A few Mourning Doves manned different lampposts. No sign of my mockingbird, but he usually stays out of the way when the Scrub Jay is around.

Those who long for the peace of the country after the hubbub of the city can still find little pieces of it. Just look and be alert. That's important in city life, for both self-protection and the pleasure of a quick treat of nature.

Over Winco, a crow was descending on a raven. It was after

that I saw the mockingbird descending on a cat running across the street. Justice for the birds!

If I'd just been mulling over my own problems, or complaining about potholes in the road, crazy drivers, and politics, I'd never have noticed these treats, even though they happened right in front of me. What else may I have missed just because I wasn't alert? Like the children of Israel, the generation that missed out on going into the Promised Land simply because of their complaining.

As I apply this principle of being alert and looking for blessings, not problems, then somehow, some way, I can expect a surprise blessing. "Seek and ye shall find."

Too many get stuck in the complainer's rut and see only the pit they've fallen in. Look up! The sky is more beautiful than the hole. This morning, it was decorated with a peachy moon slowly going down in the west. The pretty color might have been due to the unpleasant smoke still in the air from distant fires still burning.

On my walk this morning, I met a neighbor, Pam. She said she has been watching me for years, and seeing me out walking has been an encouragement to her. She sees me and says, "Go for it, girl!" It's nice to know I've been an encouragement and never even known it.

Who else is looking at me?

CHAPTER 53

God's Object Lessons

God's Word was not written to animals (though many are mentioned in it) or for animals (though it says much about how man should treat or regard animals), but to humans. Animals did not disobey their Maker. Humans did. The animals, birds, bugs, and insects are object lessons to us, many instances of which are recorded in the Bible, as God seeks to teach us wisdom and draw us closer to Himself in fellowship.

We are reminded that we have dominion over the creatures of the earth. What does "dominion" mean? One of the dictionary's definitions is "supreme authority." Does "authority over" not include "responsibility for"? Just as a parent has dominion over a child, that clearly includes caring for the child and training him to care for himself or herself. And protecting them from whatever accident might harm them.

Are we not responsible for animals in a similar way? We do not need to train all of them, for some are born knowing how to care for themselves. Some of the lowest forms (like fleas) scatter and survive on their own. Others need the parent to guide—even if for just a while (like bears).

CHAPTER 54

Experiencing God Secondhand

Do you have time to sit down and travel through the trails of another person's mind? A writer is opening up trails for the reader to follow. Besides opening himself to the possibility of derision and cruelty, there is the possibility that the writer will do harm to the reader. If all he is doing is wasting the time of the reader, causing him to wander in fields of vanity when he could be doing more profitable things both for himself and others, then who is most at fault: the writer for leading the reader into vanity or the reader for not recognizing his folly?

A good writer is one who triggers another mind to think and see for itself, not just blindly follow the rhetoric of something that caught the writer's eye for a moment. The works of C. S. Lewis cause me to escape but also to think, and even when I'm not trying to think, an image of Narnia will pop into my head and make some experience I'm having more understandable. Of course, scripture is like that. The greatest of human writers can't compare to the influence of scripture in permeating and influencing the thoughts of man. And the greatest of writers give evidence of scripture in their works. If I want to read something that will have a positive influence on my writing, I can't go wrong by sticking with the Bible.

Reading Annie Dillard's *Pilgrim at Tinker Creek* is like taking a walk through a forest and enjoying all of nature's variety. Adam and Eve must have done things like this back in the Garden of

Eden—or even after. I imagine that after the Fall, they didn't have God walking with them as much. They had to experience Him more secondhand through His creation. Reading Dillard's experiences is like experiencing nature secondhand, which can be satisfying if you are close enough to nature to put down your book, step out of your door, and venture into a field or garden.

Yesterday, two of the Wildlife Heritage Foundation workers were going through the dry weeds and grasses of the vernal pool, taking stock of what was there. I went out to chat with them as I saw them returning to their truck in the parking lot. They showed me a dead, dry praying mantis in a plastic bag, which led me to tell them about Annie Dillard's account of the praying mantis biting off the head of her partner after mating with him.

I love Dillard's wonder with creation, the awe of mysteries that cannot be understood. I'm barely into her book, just savoring it slowly. She is so inspiring. She did get the Pulitzer Prize for her work. She says, "Seeing is ... a matter of verbalization." Unless she calls attention to what passes before her eyes, she won't see it.

When I write something, then read it years later, the memory flashes vividly in my mind.

CHAPTER 55
Grass Withers

I am looking out on the vernal pool, which has just been getting drier and drier for the past three months. No birds are coming to eat the bugs because no bugs are there (at least in great abundance, except for ants). It is an illustration of 1 Peter 1:24–25:

- "For all flesh is as grass." Yes, the scientists, scholars, theologians, philosophers.
- "And the glory of man as the flower of grass." Their writings, accomplishments, and influences are brilliant and glorious.
- "The grass withereth, the flower thereof falleth away." This glory does change continually as new science discoveries invalidate and outdate some of the views of Darwin. (Some? I'm being kind.)
- "But the Word of our Lord endureth forever." This is the Word they mocked. It is still around, standing the test of time and criticism, while their works are fading, being apologized for, updated, and continually replaced.

I look out on this field of dry grass and remember that this is "all flesh." So, instead of swallowing myself with earthly endeavors that fade, I need to concentrate on the eternal, the Word of God, and the wisdom it can give me for living out my short time on this earth.

CHAPTER 56

The End-Time Big Bang

To balance knowledge we have faith and hope. Knowledge can be depressing if you have no faith or hope. In 1 Peter, he starts off talking about faith and hope, then reminds us of the living hope we have through Christ Jesus. We are kept by God through faith that is going to be tested.

Then his end-time cautions. "The end of all things is at hand" (1 Peter 4:7) and "time has come for judgment to begin at the house of God ... what will be the end of those who do not obey the gospel of God?" (1 Peter 4:17).

This is left as an unanswered question. The Bible was not written to answer all of our questions but to steer us in the right direction of the important questions and keep us seeking.

Peter balances these words of faith and hope when he refers to "knowledge" (2 Peter 1). He speaks of "knowledge of God and of Jesus" and what that knowledge has given us (2 Peter 1:2–4). This knowledge may not be enough, and he warns that some have escaped the pollutions of the world through this knowledge—but then turned back again and ended up worse off than they were to begin with (2 Peter 2:20–21)

There will be scoffers in these last days (1 Peter 3:3). Every time you turn on the TV or listen to the news, somebody is scoffing at something. The learned are scoffing at the unlearned, the right is scoffing at the left, the poor are scoffing at the rich, Calvinists are scoffing at Armenians, gays are scoffing at straights, on an on, back and forth. All society is ready to explode at the drop of a hat.

The "Big bang" is the term used by the "scientific community" to describe the beginning of the universe. But according to Peter (2 Peter 3:10), that's a better description of its end. He tells us that in scripture are "some things hard to understand" (2 Peter 3:16). He doesn't pretend he can understand all things that only God can understand. It takes faith.

CHAPTER 57

Choose Your Idol: Hollywood or Technology

Moses had struggles with the Children of Israel and their desires to have a harmless god they could touch and see like the gods of the people around them, not this invisible God that was powerful and frightening. What are the idols of today's culture?

Movie stars are commonly called idols, and no one thinks a thing about it. The dictionary says "idol" is a symbol of a deity used as an object of worship. What is worship? "To honor or reverence as a divine being," says Webster's.

Thinking of the attitude of most Americans toward Hollywood and its idols, "worship" in the sense of occupying their time, money, and minds—as well as their voices in praising particular actors—is certainly the right word.

Moses warned the Israelites (Deuteronomy 7:4) against the people's idols: "For they shall turn away thy son from following me." Why was God so strict with Israel? "Thou art an holy people" (Deuteronomy 7:6). Obviously they didn't want to be holy and bucked against it.

As we look at ourselves, Christians in America today, what should our attitude toward Hollywood be? We've got two examples to choose from.

First is Moses (Deuteronomy 7:25–26), where idols were to be an abomination to be detested and destroyed.

Then we have the apostle Paul, the first missionary to the Gentiles, who found the Athenians totally given to idolatry. He called attention to their altar to the Unknown God they worshipped ignorantly. That's who he wanted to tell them about (Acts 17).

An attitude like Paul's in a culture oversaturated with Hollywood would seem wise. I've heard a few preachers use incidents from popular movies to illustrate points in their sermons. Movies are something most people can relate to, unlike farming, fishing, and shepherding, which are the basis of understanding many of Christ's parables and teachings.

The secret is not that Christians know movies so well. It's that they know scripture so well that when they see something that illustrates a point, they recognize it. Christians just need skill in applying God's Word to their lives and the world around them. To do that, they have to know God's Word first.

In this age of technology, we are getting further and further from nature, when a sermon illustrated by movie scenes from well-known movies will get across a point that a nature parable will not.

Technology could be labeled an idol, but it's the basis of communication. You can't give the gospel to the Chinese if you don't speak their language.

CHAPTER 58

Bible Binoculars

Before sunrise, and before my morning walk, I stepped outside to see how the world felt. Redding has had record high temperatures this year (2017) and now more than fifty-seven days of triple digits. It's been warm even through the night and into morning before it gets even hotter as the day progresses. Smoke has been blowing in from the various fires in the area, and everything has been hazy and gray.

This morning, I lifted my eyes to the south and saw the belt of Orion! It's been a long time since I've seen stars, and Orion is my favorite constellation. I ran back inside to get my binoculars, and then I anchored my back against the doorpost to hold the binoculars steadier (sometimes a problem with more high-powered binoculars, to say nothing of aging hands trembling). Ah! The feast of stars I saw! Glittering, sparkling, all around those basic few stars that unaided eyes are limited to. Worlds! Galaxies! To think that just yesterday all of this was blocked by minute particles of smoke. Of course, if I hadn't looked up, I wouldn't have seen it now. So, as well as the blinders blocking the view (the smoke), the eyes needed to look up. Of course, the binoculars really opened the view. All too often, we humans never look up. Our eyes are focused on a little box in our hand or a screen on a wall or desk.

Comparing the Bible to binoculars, and seeing life through its wisdom, is to gain far more from life than just momentary pleasures. These binoculars (the Bible) help you realize that life is far more than what you see before you in the moment. Indeed, it is far more than you can even begin to understand, and the mysteries of God and the universe have no end, in spite of how much is discovered every day.

It gives insight for today's living as well as hope for tomorrow.

CHAPTER 59

High Smoke and the Birds

Imagine an oak leaf. Instead of falling to the ground, it begins zipping in and out of the other stationary leaves, up and down and all around the oak tree. That's what it seems like as I watch the little green and white hummingbird make its way around the oak. Now it's gone. I think.

Does the high smoke content of the air tell the birds to be quick and cautious? And is that why the Acorn Woodpecker is staying close to the ground like a beetle on the trunk of an oak instead of flying from cache to cache on the top of his telephone poles (where I usually see him)?

Something flew by so quickly. Was it a tiny bird or great big bug? There have been lots of dragonflies this year, like fancy earrings bouncing and flashing through the air.

Just when I decide all is still and quiet and the birds have flown, I see movement. A Western Bluebird in the oaks of the church parking lot. Then out of sight just as quickly. How many birds have I missed when I pause to write? They probably watch me, and when I look down, they dart around. I'll just have to stop writing and look.

CHAPTER 60

Interruptions: A Bird and a Soul

I went to check on the birdbath under the oak behind the library. (Did I tell you my birdbath was just a garbage lid that I fill and refill with water periodically?) With the vernal pool gone, I wanted to give the birds a source of water. Some kind of scum was floating on it, so I emptied it, washing it out with the hose, and set it upright against the oak to dry out. The hose didn't have ...

Interruption!

As I wrote the above, from my secluded chair behind the library, a young man suddenly passed directly between the birdbath and me. A little Nuttall's Woodpecker was pecking around it, wondering where the water had gone.

"Wait a minute!" I called to the young man.

He looked startled. He didn't know whether to stop or run.

"Didn't you leave a sack of clothes when you were here a few months ago?" I recognized him right away as the young fellow in the security footage from when the college had been broken into (and nothing taken, though many tools laying around could have been easily snatched).

After I'd heard about the break-in, I walked around the grounds seeking my own clues. I'd found a clean black canvas sack with clean, neatly folded clothes dumped on the ground around it. (Did the police do that?) I gathered them up and kept the sack in the back of the library.

He stopped, and we talked. His name was Brent (he said). He

told me the story of how he came to be homeless at this time, and he showed me the Bible he carried with him.

He told me about his rough life and disappointed expectations with his family, and I told him to read Psalm 27. "Especially verse 10: 'When my father and mother forsake me then the LORD will take me up.'"

I gave him his sack of clothes, and we parted. Who knows where he went?

CHAPTER 61

Bird-Watching and Scripture Memory

Not a bird in sight. Occasionally I hear a call or chirp.

I sit and focus on leaves in the oak tree, practicing using my binoculars to focus on some particular leaf as if it were a bird. I sit and focus on leaves. Perfectly still, no breeze today.

I select a leaf and see how quickly I can find it with my binoculars. Then, right where I am looking, a little yellow bird lands. A Lesser Goldfinch? No. A Yellow-rumped Warbler! I thought I'd been hearing a warbler for a few days now, but I just hadn't sighted one. I can't trust my ears with mockingbirds around.

Just think. All my years of poring through bird handbooks, learning the sizes of markings of birds I'd never seen, all paid off in this one glorious moment I might have totally missed. Those two little birds look so much alike—the same colors arranged in different patterns, and both the colors of the yellowing oak leaves with the sunlight dancing in the leaves.

It's like memorizing scripture. The greatest satisfaction doesn't come from knowing it; it comes from getting to use it. All the drudgery of memorizing pays off in the moment of being able to apply God's Word to a life situation. Planned or unplanned, ready.

CHAPTER 62
Moses and the Wilderness

Moses was well acquainted with the wilderness. Having fled the civilization of Egypt, he spent forty years tending flocks in the desert. By then, he was prepared to lead God's people (were sheep as stubborn and prone to stray as these people?) through the wilderness to the Promised Land. Even then, he had his times alone with God, especially on a mountain. Deuteronomy 32 is the song Moses spoke to the children of Israel as a reminder of what their God had done for them:

> For the LORD's portion is His people: Jacob is the lot of his inheritance.
> He found him in a desert place, and in the waste howling wilderness; he led him about, he instructed him …
> As an eagle stirreth up her nest, fluttereth over her young, spreadeth abroad her wings, taketh them, beareth them on her wings:
> So the LORD alone did lead him …
> (Deuteronomy 32: 9–12)

As Moses speaks of the eagle, anyone who has seen one spread its wings and rise into the air can picture that power and the wonder of the promise:

So the LORD alone led him ... he made him ride in
the heights of the earth. (Deuteronomy 32:13)

Someone who did not know the eagle or the wilderness could
not have as effectively described the LORD's leading and caring for
His own.

As we become occupied with technology, with creating our
own virtual worlds, it is taking us away from the wilderness and
what it has to offer. It seems to give stress, not peace.

CHAPTER 63

Just Another Day, or Why I Enjoy Nature

Yesterday, I identified a total of sixteen species while I was trying to write in my journal and not watch birds. If I want to attract birds, maybe I should ignore them and write as much as possible.

The little flock of sparrows pecking in the school playground across the street are at least two different species. The bullies who try to chase others away (it seems) are the White-crowned Sparrows. The ones with the streaked breast and yellow eyebrow are Savannah Sparrows.

A few birds have been singing to me from behind leaf cover, but they won't show themselves. One showed off his speed skills by doing a loop in the air in front of me, then darting around the building out of my sight. Aviators could take a few lessons from him.

I'm also seeing (I'm not really watching, I'm too familiar with them) the starlings who hang out on the metal tubular arms of the telephone pole on the corner. The Acorn Woodpecker claims the top of that pole, and only when he's gone do the starlings dare to park there.

My eyes are getting blurry, and my fingers are getting cold. But if I go inside, I won't see the trees that help me organize my thoughts or the birds that fly by like fresh ideas sparking my mind to keep working, with the promise of some unexpected drama if I just sit still and wait. To top it all off, as the sun rises above the smoke and haze the winds have brought, even the dullest oak trees have a glorious golden glow, and the dry grass scatters amber jewels. If you're not looking, you won't see it.

There is a little bird tweeting at me from a bush not five feet away. I can see the leaves around him shaking, but not him. I'll just ignore him and try to write—maybe then he'll show himself.

CHAPTER 64

A Hunter Told Me

"I have felt closer to God out in the wild than in any church I ever went to."

Being close to God is certainly an important, if not supreme, purpose of our lives. In the wilderness, away from the world and its distractions and entrapments, the mind can absorb the peace, readjust its own thoughts, and open to new thoughts inspired by nature and its Creator.

Yet it was in the wilderness that Jesus was led by the Spirit to be tempted of the devil (Matthew 4:1). The devil is also familiar with the wilderness. And not just the wilderness of the plain, but the glories of mountain heights that so few know since climbing is dangerous and takes incredible skill (at least for humans) and training. The devil promised Jesus all the kingdoms of the world if he would worship him. Did the devil know that Jesus was the Creator of all these things? Was he just as mystified as the Jews were about this upstart prophet from Galilee? This must have been his first clue that Jesus was someone to keep an eye on since He didn't yield to the temptation of power. Few can resist that.

I think again of that hunter who felt close to God in nature. Was his purpose to get close to God—or just to get out of church? Who am I to judge? That the church is full of imperfect people with glaring shortcomings is no more a reason not to go to church than to not go to the hospital because it's full of sick people.

Believers are reminded: Consider one another—to provoke

unto love and good works (Hebrews 10:24–25). Do not just provoke (some stop there) but love and do good works. Then it goes on: Not forsaking the assembling of ourselves together (as the manner of some is) but exhorting one another. How plain can you get? We need the church, and it needs us. Some may choose a club or tavern. Jesus designed the church and set its patterns in motion with His disciples.

CHAPTER 65

Nectar

Professor Phillips (who teaches English Grammar and Composition here at Shasta Bible College) was remarking to me at how amazed he was by the little hummingbird, faster even than sparrows that seem bulky in comparison. It needs that nectar of the flower to give it energy for its daily tasks.

"So the Christian needs the nectar of the Word of God to accomplish their tasks for the Lord." He was referring to the roadblock I seemed to have come to in the writing of my book.

"So this is what 'writer's block' is?" I said.

"Go fill up on the Word, and you will be reinvigorated to go on with your work," he said.

It was just the advice I needed!

I thanked him and came straight to my notebook. I must quit putting off the things I can't finish and just do what I can. Step by step. Beginning with drawing nectar from the Word, the source that will never wither and die as the grass and flowers of this world, for it is the Word that stands forever.

To anyone who scoffs at it, I say, "It's been around longer than you have—and it will still be around when you are gone and your words are forgotten."

CHAPTER 66

Back to the Word

Hummingbird's poem:

Back to the Word!
Says the hummingbird.
Don't make John Muir's mistake of
Worshipping nature
And not the Creator.
My inspiration comes from nectar
Of the flower that fades.
Yours is the
Everlasting Word.
Forever.

CHAPTER 67
Dangerous World for Birds and Children

Sweet little birds certainly live in a dangerous world. They have to learn to protect themselves or die. How can they protect themselves? Lions use their strength, claws, and teeth. Birds don't have those abilities, but they have flight. Lions don't have that.

Birds still have to be cautious and not carelessly dance into a dangerous situation. They examine an area before they land there. Geese will circle a pond several times, taking it all in before they hydroplane in. Even then, they stay on alert (especially designated ones, it seems).

We want to teach our children to be alert like the birds and take off from situations that could get dangerous. There might be nothing wrong with the neighborhood kids crawling through the blackberry patch, but are they hiding something there they don't want grown-ups to see?

Sometimes, the parent has to let them make their own decisions and suffer the consequences. Like the bird that didn't fly when it could, they may have to learn the consequences of their own decisions without their parents hovering around. God lets His creatures and His children make bad choices. Why do you suppose He does that? It started back in the Garden of Eden.

CHAPTER 68

Journey of Life: One Day at a Time

Can it be said that he who has prepared for the journey of the day has prepared for the journey of life? Even a long journey can only be traveled one day at a time. If that day is not prepared for, both physically and spiritually, that journey can falter and fail.

But even if it does falter, if the traveler should fall into a pit, a new day can start again with preparation. The goal for a new day will be learning how to climb up the side of a slippery, rocky pit. Learning may involve slipping a few more times, but it will come. There may be a purpose for being in this pit anyway: being saved from some danger farther along the trail that more training was necessary for or to be a help to someone else stranded in another pit.

Yesterday, I was questioning whether I wanted to write. Now I know I do because I teach myself while I do it. Writing makes me more aware of how much I do not know rather than revealing what I do know.

I take some comfort in Proverbs 20:24: "Man's goings are of the LORD: how can a man then understand his own way?"

CHAPTER 69

Journey of Life Draws to a Close

As one ages, and the end of life's journey draws closer, there is both conscious and unconscious preparation for it. The mind begins to fail and forget, and others must step up to do the tasks that once this one did—or leave them undone. Thus, the traveler and those being left behind are all being prepared for his departure.

Of course, some departures are unexpected, and the departed and those left alive were both unprepared. The adjustment to such departures for those left behind is often difficult. Neither is easy. With the unexpected death or the expected one, it is the living who have to deal with it.

Is losing a beloved partner harder to bear than losing one who was a burden? Not necessarily. The Lord is the Author of each life, and He has His purpose in the load each must bear, as in the parable of the talents handed out to the servants.

Right now, I'm just jabbering, hoping some great insight will come to me as I write and be a fitting conclusion to the thoughts that have been tumbling in my head.

But as I sit here behind the library, distracted by a Lesser Goldfinch that landed on my contrived birdbath, and hearing another bird twittering in a nearby bush at the same time, I'm just enjoying the peace and life all around me.

Death is something most of the living do not prepare for. It's the most inevitable fact of life. How do we prepare? Financially, some provide for their families in the event they should die. But that's not providing for *themselves*. Even buying a beautiful coffin and erecting a glorious monument is no more preparing for death than an unexpected miscarriage is preparation for death.

The Bible reveals more that can be depended on about death than any other source, but it doesn't tell us as much as we'd like to know.

Why? God wants us to live for life, not death. It will come soon enough; this life is a vapor that comes and passes away. We will be judged by how we lived our lives and not how we prepared to die. The everlasting life promised in John 3:16 to "whosoever believeth" is the best way to prepare. Whenever I doubted God's love for someone like me, that "whosoever believeth" was the promise to which I cling.

CHAPTER 70

An Approaching Wildfire

Traffic in the streets is normal, and people are going about their everyday business. What would suggest that anything threatening was about to happen? All summer, this region had been on "fire alert." That's normal. The skyline had lost the clear, clean sharpness of spring, and it was so hazy the surrounding mountains couldn't be seen. The air smelled smoky, and a layer of ash coated everything. No one stayed outside to breathe this air if they didn't have to. Is that why not too many birds are around? The few that appear dart quickly about their business, then are gone, like the people.

If fire actually comes here, what do we do? Grab what we can and flee! One year, the evacuation line came to the edge of the campus. The students could choose what they wanted to do: stay or flee. The girls packed into cars and took off for a safety zone. The boys chose to stay and grabbed hoses and shovels to fight any attacking flame or spark.

These wildfires that threaten destruction certainly seem to picture the judgment of God. Jeremiah warned the hardheaded, disobedient people of the consequences of their sin:

> Flee from the midst of Jerusalem ... for disaster
> appears out of the north and great destruction ...
> violence and plundering are heard in her ... from
> the least of them even to the greatest of them,

everyone is given to covetousness; and from the prophet even to the priest, everyone deals falsely. (Jeremiah 6:1–13)

Everything God did to Israel is a warning to the rest of the world. The same fate would certainly await a nation that claimed to be "under God" and had "In God We Trust" on its money.

How can we live in such an ominous world without being overcome with fear and depression? We "consider the raven," which doesn't worry about tomorrow's meal, but just faces today's needs. So we should live day by day trusting a God we know will provide what we need when we need it—be that food or courage.

CHAPTER 71

Letter to My Child in a Darkening World

The world you face today and in which you have to raise your children is full of dangers and temptations beyond what I ever imagined in my day—far worse even than when I raised you such a short while ago. With technology to make life easy, you are deprived of the skills my parents had drilled into them by their parents and tried to drill into me, and which I made a pretense of trying to drill into you: discipline, perseverance, and commitment. Good family and dependable friends surrounded us. People talk about "the good old days," as if moving time back would solve today's problems. Giving you the world we had is not the answer. It is what brought us where we are now.

Your light may be dimmer than mine is, but your world is darker. Therefore, your light seems brighter and reaches people who would never come near the floodlights of a church.

God has a different path for you than the one He has for me—though it's taken me a long time to figure this out. Many of the hazards are the same, but many are things I would never have dreamed of in a nightmare. What I've sought to warn you to be cautious about, you have gone charging toward with all your energy. So now you know firsthand about these dangers.

Looking back, I wish I hadn't concentrated so much on the "no-no's" and focused more on the "yes-yes" issues: How I enjoy the workmanship of the Creator and His design in the birds and the stars. How I look forward to meeting and knowing Him even better someday.

For now, His letters are enlightening, comforting, and precious. After reading the Bible a hundred times, I'm still learning new things from it every day. Spending eternity with the Author of this book is the greatest joy I can imagine.

Then again, that's not something I could have taught you. It's something you'd have to discover for yourself.

CHAPTER 72

Light in This Darkening World

A s night draws on, the darkness comes slowly. The eye adjusts, and I can continue activity long after the sun has set. Any feeble light can be blinding when you've been self-sufficient in the darkness for a while. It's easier to stay outside in the dark than to adjust to inside light.

Some birds, like the owl, are designed for nocturnal living. They can avoid regular daytime predators and exploit prey that can't see them.

Owls aren't evil because they function in the darkness, but Jesus warned that men love darkness rather than light because their deeds are evil (John 3:19).

Blindness is a deep darkness. The warning that the god of this world hath blinded the minds of them that believe not (1 Corinthians 4:4) reminds us we are in a world of blind people who think they see. We are still to let our light shine. The devil may blind people, but it's God who heals the eyes and the soul. And the entrance of thy word gives light (Psalm 119:130)

Jesus said, "I am the light of the world" (John 8:12), but told His disciples, "Ye are the light of the world" (Matthew 5:14). The Philippians were warned by Paul in the evil culture they lived in:

> That ye may be blameless and harmless ... in the
> midst of a crooked and perverse nation among

whom ye shine as lights in the world. (Philippians 2:15)

As the sun sets, and the glory of the sunset fades, darkness threatens to swallow everything, when little pinpricks of light begin to appear. The stars! They were there even while the sun was marching across the sky, but not until the sun had passed were the glories of these lesser lights apparent. When the darkness is strongest, as any stargazer knows, these lights shine brightest just before dawn. Shine—the dawn is coming!

CHAPTER 73

Faith in a Darkening World

In what should we put our faith in these troublesome times?

Mankind? Some react to a story of goodness in the midst of the flood of bad news with the remark: "That restores my faith in fellow man!" Not realistic. With ninety-nine points against and one point for, you'll go with the team with only one point? Humanity has proven it's not worthy of faith.

Faith in ourselves? I've let myself down enough to know that faith in myself is a joke. The heart is deceitful above all things and desperately wicked (Jeremiah 17:9). We can't trust even ourselves. Sounds hopeless.

Religion? Religious people are some of the greatest deceivers of all. The Bible even warns to watch for the false prophets "among you." Even if they are sincere, maybe they've been fooled by deceivers.

God? Okay—which one? Alcoholics Anonymous members are to choose their "higher power," and with paganism being revived, there are countless ones to choose from. Which one do you want? Are they all equally good—or is there some way to determine which might be best?

Israel's God and Baal were put to the test in the days of Elijah.

Who is God anyway? Whatever you define him to be? Everyone has their own idea, and they all describe something different. Why don't we let Him tell us who He is?

Let's focus on the one God of the Bible, who in the beginning ...

created the heaven and the earth (Genesis 1:1). From that first verse of the Bible onward, it describes this God and His dealings with mankind. Humans let Him down again and again (it's recorded there), but He remained faithful and kept every promise He made. Even the promise of judgment when the time came.

Is this the God you are considering putting your faith in? That is the question of the ages, and each person must decide for himself or herself.

Okay, so you've made your decision. This God of the Bible is the one you want to trust, indeed, have put your trust in. But you find yourself crying with the father of the afflicted child, Lord, I believe! Help thou mine unbelief (Mark 9:24).

Ravens can teach us faith. Job tells how God provides for them (Job 38:41), and Jesus reminded His followers:

> Consider the ravens ... God feedeth them so He
> will provide for you. (Luke 12:24)

We think we are in control of our lives and their circumstances, and our faith fails when things don't go as we planned. We blame God first, not realizing that our faith has shifted from Him to ourselves. Of course it will fail.

Birds know they aren't in control. They're not worried about tomorrow's meal or safety. Only right now. And they're not worried, just alert and ready.

RECOMMENDED HANDBOOKS

American Museum of Natural History Birds of North America (New York: DK Publishing, Rev. ed. 2016). A good "coffee table book." Illustrations larger than the standard handbook, which help in identifying details on a bird. "Similar Species" and other features help in identifying birds.

National Geographic Field Guide to the Birds of North America (latest edition). A good handbook to begin with. Just flip through the pages and begin learning the birds. Suddenly you'll notice one you've seen before. Then, another time, you'll see one outside that you remembered seeing in the book. Where was that? And thus begins your adventure of bird identification.